THE POCKET
INTERPRETER
CHINESE

by Lydia Chen and Ying Bian

FOREIGN LANGUAGES PRESS BEIJING

First Printing 1988
Second Printing 1990

ISBN 0-8351-2320-0
ISBN 7-119-00557-X

Copyright 1988 by Foreign Languages Press

Published by Foreign Languages Press
24 Baiwanzhuang Road, Beijing, China

Printed by Sino-British Printing Corporation
3 Chegongzhuang Road, Beijing, China

Distributed by
China International Book Trading Corporation
(Guoji Shudian)
P.O. Box 399, Beijing, China

Printed in the People's Republic of China

Editorial Consultant: Shen Jun
Researchers: Yang Dan, Tong Xiuying, Zhang Hongyan,
Li Jun, Wang Jingzhen

Cover Illustration by Miao Yintang
Text Illustrations by Miao Yintang, Tang Yu
Design by Richard Hentz

Contents

SIDEBARS

Introduction

Going to China is a dream come true for many Westerners. In recent years, the opportunities for business, vacation, and educational trips have increased rapidly. Without some knowledge of the Chinese language, however, you will find yourself either confined to hotels and offices where English is spoken or totally dependent on the services of an interpreter. To help you have some independence while in China, *The Pocket Interpreter: Chinese* provides the sentence patterns you will most often need and the vocabulary with which you can create new sentences. In addition, each chapter includes brief information which will help you better understand the Chinese people, their society, and their culture.

The design of this book is to offer basic sentences upon which other sentences can be patterned, rather than attempt to provide specific phrases for every situation the China traveler could possibly encounter. You can use this book effectively by mastering the basic patterns, such as "...*zài nǎr?*" (Where is...?) and "*Yǒu méi yǒu...?*" (Do you have...?), and referring to the dictionary for the specific words you need to make the sentence you want. The twenty-two sentence patterns introduced in Chapter One recur often in the subsequent chapters. By recognizing the patterns each time they reappear, you will soon be able to use them on your own.

In the patterns, the words for which substitutions can be made have been bracketed in both the English and Chinese pinyin versions. Thus you will know where to replace a given word with one that is more suited to your needs. For example, if the English sentence is "Where is the (zoo)?" the

corresponding Chinese would be *"(Dòngwùyuán) zài nǎr?"*
Seeing that *dòngwùyuán* is the equivalent of zoo, you could
then look up another word in the dictionary, such as museum, and substitute its Chinese equivalent, *bówùguǎn*, in
the given sentence. "Where is the museum?" would thus be
"Bówùguǎn zài nǎr?"

The Chinese words in this book have been spelled according to the pinyin system, the official transliteration of Putonghua used in the People's Republic of China. Putonghua,
also known as Mandarin, is the national dialect of China.
Based on a northern dialect, similar to that of Beijing, it is
used in national broadcasts and taught in public schools
throughout China. When among people of their own locality,
however, Chinese still speak their own local dialects, which
vary greatly from region to region. In Guangzhou, for example, you will hear people around you speaking Cantonese,
which bears almost no resemblence to Putonghua. Neverthe-
less, Putonghua is generally understood and you can use it
wherever you go in China.

Since most Chinese do not read pinyin easily, the phrases
here have also been given in Chinese characters, or *Hànzì*.
The *Hànzì* used are the simplified characters of China, which
are slightly different from the traditional characters used in
Taiwan, Hong Kong, Singapore, and other places. People
who know the traditional characters can usually figure out
the simplified forms by context. If you have difficulty pro-
nouncing a Chinese word or phrase, you can point to the
accompanying *Hànzì* and ask the Chinese with whom you
wish to communicate to read it.

Every Chinese written character represents a one-syllable
word. Many Chinese words, however, are compounds composed of two or more characters which each contribute
meaning to the total concept. For example, the word for
movie is *diànyǐng* (电影), composed of the words *diàn*
(electric) and *yǐng* (shadow). For ease of reading, the two
syllables have been spelled together as one word in pinyin;
in *Hànzì* they are two separate characters.

In Putonghua, each syllable is composed of an initial

sound, a final sound, and a tone. (*See charts, pp. 4-5.*) The word *diàn*, for example, has the inital sound *d*, the final sound *ian*, and the downward fourth tone (`` ` ``). You will notice that some words in pinyin do not have tonal marks above them. This is because they are unstressed syllables which should be spoken quickly in a neutral tone.

A few words, such as *yī* (one), are not always marked with the same tone when they appear in different phrases. This is because the tone of some words depends on the tone of the word following it. *Yī,* for example, should only be spoken in the first tone when it stands alone or is followed by a pause; if the next word is a first-, second-, or third-tone word, *yī* should be read as *yì*; if the next word is a fourth-tone word, *yī* should be read as *yí.* Similarly *bù* (not) should be read as *bú* when the word following it is a fourth-tone word. For convenience, *yī* and *bù* have been marked in this book according to the tones in which they should be read within the phrase given, not as they are listed in the dictionary.

The tone, or inflection, of a Chinese word is just as important as its pronunciation. This aspect of speaking Chinese is the most difficult for English speakers to learn. In English, the tone of a word varies with the mood of the sentence; in Chinese, the tone stays the same whether the sentence is a question, exclamation, or matter-of-fact statement. Mood is indicated by stress on certain words, rather than inflection. To use the wrong tone in a Chinese word would be the equivalent of saying "cat" for "dog" in English.

The key to learning a new language is repetition. Begin by practicing a few simple phrases, such as *nǐhǎo* (hello) and *xièxie* (thank you), which you can use many times a day. Then build up to the useful phrases presented in Chapter One. To perfect your Putonghua, ask a Chinese friend to help you with your pronunciations and tones. Also, reinforce your grasp of the language by listening and looking. Be on the alert for the commonly heard phrases and often seen signs presented at the end of each chapter. With these thoughts in mind, a positive outlook, and book in hand, *Yí lù shùnfēng* (may good winds follow you)!

Pronunciation Guide

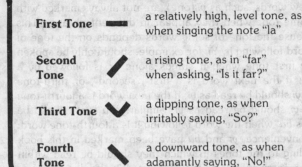

TONES

First Tone	—	a relatively high, level tone, as when singing the note "la"
Second Tone	/	a rising tone, as in "far" when asking, "Is it far?"
Third Tone	∨	a dipping tone, as when irritably saying, "So?"
Fourth Tone	\	a downward tone, as when adamantly saying, "No!"

INITIAL SOUNDS

b, d, f, g, h, j, k, l, m, n, p, s, t, w, y	roughly the same as in English
ch, sh	as in English, but curl the tongue up toward the roof of the mouth while pronouncing the "ch" or "sh" sound
c	ts as in ca*ts*
q	ch as in *cheese*
r	zhr, like in plea*s*ure
x	sh as in ban*shee*
z	ds as in car*ds*
zh	dg as in fu*dge*

4

FINAL SOUNDS

a	ah
ai	e*ye*
an	ahn
ang	ahng
ao	ow
ar	are
e	uh
ei	*eigh* as in a sl*eigh*
en	un as in r*un*
eng	ung as in h*ung*
er	cross between ar and er
i	*ee*, but after c, ch, r, s, sh, z, and zh, it is silent
ia	ee-ah (quickly, as one syllable)
ian	ee-en (quickly)
iang	ee-ahng (quickly)
iao	ee-ow (quickly)
ie	ee-eh (quickly)
in	een as in s*een*
ing	ing as in r*ing*
iong	ee-ōng (quickly)
iu	eo as in L*eo*
o	o as in *or*
ong	ōng
ou	oh
u	oo as in m*oo*
ü	cross between oo and eew, as in French t*u*
ua	wa as in *wa*sh
uai	why
uan	wahn, as in *wan*der
uang	wahng
ue	weh
ui	way
un	won
uo	wo as in *wo*re

ー1 Essentials
yī

Méi bànfă.
Tough luck
(there's no other way).

How do you even begin to learn Chinese? When you arrive in China, you will find yourself suddenly the "foreigner." At first you may feel at a loss, not knowing what to say. Gradually, by learning a few essentials, you will find your new surroundings less formidable. The sentence patterns and phrases introduced here are the ones you will draw upon most often in your travels. Master these, and you'll be able to tackle China on your own.

ESSENTIALS

22 Sentence Patterns

Can I (enter)?	*Wŏ néng bù néng (jìnqu)?*
Can you (help me)?	*Nĭ néng bù néng (bāngmáng)?*
Do you have (postcards)?	*Yŏu (míngxìnpiàn) ma?*
How much does (this) cost?	*(Zhèige) yào duōshao qián?*
I am (American).	*Wŏ shì (Mĕiguó rén).*
I am not (a movie star).	*Wŏ bú shì (diànyĭng míngxīng).*
I have (two pieces of luggage).	*Wŏ yŏu (liăng jiàn xíngli).*
I do not have (a map).	*Wŏ méi yŏu (dìtú).*
I lost my (passport).	*Wŏde (hùzhào) diū le.*
I need (to see a doctor).	*Wŏ yào (kànbìng).*
I do not need (a taxi).	*Wŏ bú yào (chūzū qìchē).*
I would like to (go to the zoo).	*Wŏ xiăng (qù dòngwùyúan).*
I would not like to (rest).	*Wŏ bù xiăng (xiūxi).*
I will stay in (Beijing) for [three days].	*Wŏ yào zài (Bĕijīng) dāi [sān tiān].*
Is there a (restaurant) nearby?	*Fùjìn yŏu (fànguăn) ma?*
Please give me (a receipt).	*Qĭng gĕi wŏ (fāpiào).*
Please help me (register).	*Qĭng bāng wŏ (dēngjì).*
This is my (shoulder bag).	*Zhè shì wŏde (bēibāo).*
This is not my (camera).	*Zhè bú shì wŏde (zhàoxiàngjī).*
When does (the bank) open?	*(Yínháng) shénme shíhòu kāimén?*
Where can I find (coffee)?	*Năr yŏu (kāfēi)?*

我能不能进去？

你能不能帮忙？

有明信片吗？

这个要多少钱？

我是美国人。

我不是电影明星。

我有两件行李。

我没有地图。

我的护照丢了。

我要看病。

我不要出租汽车。

我想去动物园。

我不想休息。

我要在北京呆三天。

附近有饭馆吗？

请给我发票。

请帮我登记。

这是我的背包。

这不是我的照相机。

银行什么时候开门？

哪儿有咖啡？

No Verb Conjugations

The easy part of learning Chinese is that there are no verb conjugations. I, you, he, we, and they, all take the same verb form. For example:

I am	*Wǒ shì*
You are	*Nǐ shì*
He is	*Tā shì*
We are	*Wǒmen shì*
You are (pl)	*Nǐmen shì*
They are	*Tāmen shì*

The pronouns are also easy to remember. The plural forms are the singular forms plus the syllable *men* (们).

Where? There!

You will find that people from different regions in China prefer different words to express the same idea, and Putonghua incorporates these variations. For example, *nǎr* and *nǎli* both mean "where" and *nàr* and *nàli*, likewise, mean "there." People in the north tend to prefer the "r" sound, as in *nǎr,* whereas southerners prefer a crisper sound, as in *nǎli.*

Negatives

The negative form of most verbs in Chinese is formed by adding the syllable *bù* (不) before the verb, almost like the word "not" in English. For example:

I know.	*Wǒ zhīdao.*
I don't know.	*Wǒ **bù** zhīdao.*

However, with the verb *yǒu* (to have), the negative is formed with the syllable *méi* (没).

continued

Where is (the post office)?	*(Yóujú) zài nǎr?*

Self-introduction

Hello.	*Nǐhǎo.*
My name is (John Smith).	*Wǒ jiào (John Smith).*
My last name is (Smith).	*Wǒ xìng (Smith).*
We're a group of (five).	*Wǒmen gòng yǒu (wǔ) gè rén.*
We're with (XYZ Company).	*Wǒmen shì (XYZ Gōngsī) de.*

Courtesies

May I have your last name, please?	*Nín guì xìng?*
Thank you.	*Xièxie.*
You're welcome.	*Bú kèqi*
Sorry.	*Duìbuqǐ.*
I'm so sorry.	*Zhēn duìbuqǐ.*
It's nothing.	*Méi guānxi.*
Excuse me (may I trouble you). . .	*Máfàn nǐ...*
Excuse me (may I ask). . .	*Qǐng wèn...*
Excuse me (sorry).	*Duìbuqǐ.*
Excuse me (make way, hate to disturb you). . .	*Láojià...*
I'm leaving now. Bye!	*Wǒ zǒu le. Zàijiàn!*

Key Phrases

What's this?	*Zhè shì shénme?*
Which one?	*Něige?*
This one.	*Zhèige.*

邮局在哪儿？

你好!

我 叫 John Smith。

我姓 Smith。

我们共有五个人。

我们是 XYZ 公司
的。

您贵姓？

谢谢。

不客气。

对不起。

真对不起。

没关系。

麻烦你……。

请问……。

对不起。

劳驾……。

我走了, 再见!

这是什么？

哪个？

这个。

| He has money. | *Tā yǒu qián.* |
| He doesn't have money. | *Tā **méi** yǒu qián.* |

Questions

Questions are formed in Chinese by adding the syllable *ma* (吗) at the end of a statement or by inserting the negative form of a verb or modifier immediately after that verb or modifier. For example:

He is your friend.
   Tā shì nǐde péngyǒu.
Is he your friend?
   *Tā shì nǐde péngyǒu **ma**?*
Is he (or is he not) your friend?
   *Tā shì **bú shì** nǐde péngyǒu?*

Measure Words

One of the most difficult skills in Chinese is the use of measure words. Every noun has a specific measure word that is used to count or refer to it, just like "gaggle" refers to geese and "pride" refers to lions in English.

The generic measure word in Chinese is *gè* (个) which can refer to almost anything. However, use of specific measure words is more proper. The proper measure word for books, for example, is *běn* (tome or edition). Whenever books are mentioned, *běn* precedes *shū* (book):

one book	*yì běn shū*
this book	*zhèi běn shū*
five books	*wǔ běn shū*
which book?	*něi běn shū?*

For a list of common measure words, refer to Appendix B on page 205.

ESSENTIALS

That one.	*Nèige.*
Right.	*Duì.*
Wrong.	*Bú duì.*
Enough.	*Goù le.*
Just right.	*Zhèng hǎo.*
How far?	*Duōyuǎn?*
How long (duration)?	*Duōjiǔ?*
How much?	*Duōshao?*
What time is it?	*Xiànzài jǐdiǎn le?*

Bridging the Gap

I don't understand.	*Wǒ bù míngbái.*
Please speak more slowly.	*Qǐng shuō de màn yìdiǎn.*
Please point to it.	*Qǐng zhǐ gěi wǒ kàn.*
Will you please repeat that?	*Qǐng chóngfù yí biàn.*
Could you write it down?	*Nǐ néng xiě xià lai ma?*
How do you pronounce this?	*Zhèige zěnme niàn?*
What does this mean?	*Zhè shì shénme yìsi?*

Emergencies

Help!	*Jiùmìng!*
Call the police.	*Kuài jiào jǐngchá.*
Get a doctor.	*Kuài jiào yīshēng lái.*
There's a fire.	*Nà biān qǐ huǒ le.*
There's been an accident.	*Nà biān chūshì le.*

那个。

对。

不对。

够了。

正好。

多远?

多久?

多少?

现在几点了?

我不明白。

请说得慢一点。

请指给我看。

请重复一遍。

你能写下来吗?

这个怎么念?

这是什么意思?

救命!

快叫警察。

快叫医生来。

那边起火了。

那边出事了。

Past Tense

The past tense of a verb in Chinese is made by adding the syllable *le* (了) immediately after the verb or at the very end of the sentence. For example:

I'm going.	*Wǒ qù.*
I went.	*Wǒ qù **le**.*
I went shopping.	*Wǒ qù mǎi dōngxi **le**.*

Zheige or Zhege?

You might wonder why there is an inconsistency in the pronunciation, and pinyin spelling, of *zhè* (这), meaning "this"; *nà* (那), meaning "that"; and *nǎ* (哪), meaning "which." When the word following these indicators is a measure word, then *zhè* is often pronounced *zhèi*; *nà* is pronounced *nèi* or *nè*; and *nǎ* is pronounced *něi*. For example:

this one	*zhège, zhèige*
that one	*nàge, nèige, nège*
which one?	*nǎge? něige?*

What You'll Hear

bù hǎo	no good
bù xíng	not okay; doesn't work
děng yì děng	wait a while
hǎo	good
kěyǐ	can be done
Méi bànfǎ.	There's no solution.
Méi yǒu.	There isn't any.
Qǐng jìn.	Please come in.
xíng	okay
Wèi!	Hello. Hey!

Signs

rùkǒu
Entrance

chūkǒu
Exit

nán cèsuǒ
Men's Toilets

nǚ cèsuǒ
Women's Toilets

gōngyòng diànhuà
Public Telephone

Travel 2 二 èr

> **Yí lù shùnfēng!**
> Bon voyage
> (good winds all the way)!

Traveling through China is fun. Making your own arrangements for travel, or being delayed in an airport or train station for several hours, however, is another story! At those times when good communication is so necessary, the phrases here can help.

TRAVEL

Asking for Information

Is there a (travel service office) nearby?

Fùjìn yǒu (lǚxíng shè) ma?

Where is the (long-distance bus station)?

(Chángtú qìchē zhàn) zài nǎr?

I'm looking for a (CITS) representative.

Wǒ xiǎng zhǎo (Guó Lǚ) de rén.

Which direction is the (train station)?

Qù (huǒchē zhàn) wǎng nǎge fāngxiàng zǒu?

Where am I supposed to go?

Wǒ gāi wǎng nǎli zǒu?

Identification

This is my (passport).

Zhè shì wǒde (hùzhào).

I'm traveling with my (wife or husband).

Wǒ shì hé wǒ (àirén) yìqǐ lái de.

We're all together.

Wǒmen dōu shì yìqǐ lái de.

I've come to (sightsee).

Wǒ shì lái (guānguāng) de.

I am going to (Shanghai).

Wǒ yào qù (Shànghǎi).

I will stay there (eight) days.

Wǒ yào zài nàli dāi (bā tiān).

Booking a Ticket

I'd like to buy (two) tickets to [Xi'an].

Wǒ yào mǎi (liǎng) zhāng qù [Xī'ān] de piào.

I'd like a (round-trip) ticket.

Wǒ yào mǎi yì zhāng (láihuí) piào.

I'd like to leave on the (9th) and return on the [17th].

Wǒ (jiǔ hào) líkāi, [shíqī hào] huílai.

How much is a (one-way) ticket to [Tianjin]?

Qù [Tiānjīn] de (dānchéng) piào duōshao qián?

Are there (soft-sleeper) tickets available?

Hái yǒu (ruǎnwò) piào ma?

International Airlines

附近有旅行社吗?

长途汽车站在哪儿?

我想找国旅的人。

去火车站往哪个方向走?

我该往哪里走?

这是我的护照。

我是和我爱人一起来的。

我们都是一起来的。

我是来观光的。

我要去上海。

我要在那里呆八天。

我要买两张去西安的票。

我要买一张来回票。

我九号离开,十七号回来。

去天津的单程票多少钱?

还有软卧票吗?

Many international airlines now land in either Shanghai or Beijing. When booking a flight, you may need to know the Chinese name for your chosen airline. Here are the names and codes of some airlines with service to China.

Air France AF	*Fǎguó Hángkōng Gōngsī* 法国航空公司
British Airways BA	*Yīngguó Hángkōng Gōngsī* 英国航空公司
Canadian Airlines Int'l CP	*Jiānádà Guójì Hángkōng Gōngsī* 加拿大国际航空公司
Japan Air Lines JI	*Rìběn Hángkōng Gōngsī* 日本航空公司
Lufthansa LH	*Xīdé Hànshā Hángkōng Gōngsī* 西德汉莎航空公司
Philippine Air Lines PR	*Fēilǜbīn Hángkōng Gōngsī* 菲律宾航空公司
Singapore Airlines SQ	*Xīnjiāpō Hángkōng Gōngsī* 新加坡航空公司
Swiss Air SR	*Ruìshì Hángkōng Gōngsī* 瑞士航空公司
Thai Airways Int'l TG	*Tàiguó Guójì Hángkōng Gōngsī* 泰国国际航空公司
United Airlines UA	*Měiguó Liánhé Hángkōng Gōngsī* 美国联合航空公司

TRAVEL

Is there a discount for (children)?	*(Xiǎoháir) piào piányi diǎn ma?*
How many stopovers are there enroute?	*Lùshàng yào tíng jǐ zhàn?*
When is the next (express train)?	*Xià cì (tèkuài) shì shénme shíjiān de?*
When is the next (ship) to [Wuhan]?	*Qù [Wǔhàn] de xià bān (chuán) shì shénme shíjiān de?*
Is there a (morning) train?	*Yǒu (zǎochén) de huǒchē ma?*
Is there an (evening) flight?	*Yǒu (wǎnshang) de hángbān ma?*
When is the last bus to (Chengde)?	*Qù (Chéngdē) de zuìhòu yí tàng qìchē shì shénme shíjiān?*
How long does it take by (train)?	*Zuò huǒchē yào duōjiǔ?*
What time should I arrive at the (airport)?	*Wǒ gāi shénme shíhòu dào (jīchǎng)?*

Waiting to Board

Where shall I go to (check in)?	*Wǒ yīnggāi dào nǎr qù (bàn shǒuxù)?*
When will flight no. (123) take off?	*(Yìbǎi èrshí sān) cì hángbān shénme shíhòu qǐfēi?*
When will train no. (45) depart?	*(Sìshí wǔ) cì huǒchē shénme shíhòu kāi?*
When will the bus to (Beidaihe) leave?	*Qù (Běidàihé) de qìchē shénme shíhòu kāi?*
When will the train to (Luoyang) leave?	*Qù (Luòyàng) de huǒchē shénme shíhòu kāi?*

小孩票便宜点吗?

路上要停几站?

下次特快是什么时间的?

去武汉的下班船是什么时间的?

有早晨的火车吗?

有晚上的航班吗?

去承德的最后一趟汽车是什么时间?

坐火车要多久?

我该什么时候到机场?

我应该到哪儿去办手续?

123 次航班什么时候起飞?

45次火车什么时候开?

去北戴河的汽车什么时候开?

去洛阳的火车什么时候开?

What Kind of Plane Is This?

To meet the growing demands of visitors and business people who travel by air, the Civil Aviation Administration of China (CAAC) has been importing foreign aircraft as well as establishing joint ventures with foreign aircraft manufacturers. In the 1950s and 1960s, China's domestic routes were flown mainly by Soviet-made airplanes. Today, many of the planes are American or Western European models. You may ask the flight attendant, *Wǒmen zuò de fēijī shì shénme xínghào de?* (What model of plane are we on?) and use the list below for reference.

Aerospace (British)	*Yǔháng Gōngsī* 宇航公司
Airbus (European)	*Kōngzhōng Kèchē* 空中客车
Antonov (Soviet)	*Ān* 安
Boeing (USA)	*Bōyīn* 波音
Ilyushin (Soviet)	*Yī'ěr* 伊尔
McDonnell Douglas (USA)	*Màikètángnà Dàogélāsī* 麦克唐纳·道格拉斯
Shorts 360 (European)	*Xiāotè Sānliùlíng* 肖特三六〇
Trident (British)	*Sānchàjǐ* 三叉戟

continued

TRAVEL

Is there any news about flight no. (789)?
(Qībǎi bāshí jiǔ) cì hángbān yǒu xiāoxi ma?

How much longer do we have to wait?
Wǒmen hái yào děng duōjiǔ?

Will I make the connecting flight?
Wǒ néng gǎnshàng xiánjiē hángbān ma?

Is there a (telephone) nearby?
Fùjìn yǒu (diànhuà) ma?

Please help me reroute my ticket.
Qǐng bāng wǒ gǎi yíxià hángbān.

All Aboard

Can you help me (store) this?
Nǐ néng bāng wǒ bǎ zhège (cún qilai) ma?

When will we arrive at (Lhasa)?
Wǒmen shénme shíhòu néng dào (Lāsà)?

How is the weather in (Chengdu)?
(Chéngdū) de tiānqì zěnmeyàng?

This (seat belt) is broken.
Zhège (ānquándài) huài le.

Can you turn on the (air-conditioning)?
Qǐng bǎ (kōngtiáo) dǎkāi, hǎo ma?

Where are we now?
Wǒmen xiànzài dào nǎli le?

What is that outside?
Wàimiàn nàge shì shénme?

What is the next station?
Xià zhàn shì nǎli?

What model of (plane) is this?
Zhège (fēijī) shì shénme xínghào?

Will you please let me know when we're almost at (Suzhou)?
Kuài dào (Sūzhōu) de shíhòu qǐng tōngzhī wǒ yíxià.

How long will we stop here?
Wǒmen yào zài zhèlǐ tíng duōjiǔ?

789 次航班有消息吗?

我们还要等多久?

我能赶上衔接航班吗?

附近有电话吗?

请帮我改一下航班。

你能帮我把这个存起来吗?

我们什么时候能到拉萨?

成都的天气怎么样?

这个安全带坏了。

请把空调打开好吗?

我们现在到哪里了?

外面那个是什么?

下站是哪里?

这个飞机是什么型号?

快到苏州的时候请通知我一下。

我们要在这里停多久?

Tuplev (Soviet)	*Tú* 图	
Twin Otter (USA)	*Shuāngshuǐtǎ* 双水獭	
Yun (PRC)	*Yùn* 运	

Good, Better, Best

Comparatives and superlatives in Chinese are formed by adding an extra word or two to the original modifier. The pattern is always the same. For example:

good	*hǎo*
better	*hǎo yìdiǎn (yìxiē)*
even better	*gèng hǎo*
best	*zuìhǎo*
fast	*kuài*
faster	*kuài yìdiǎn (yìxiē)*
even faster	*gèng kuài*
fastest	*zuìkuài*

The Chinese culture being a polite one, the first way of suggesting something more than the original is by adding *yìdiǎn* (a little) or *yìxiē* (some) after the modifier, thus implying something somewhat better but not a lot better. A stronger version of the comparative is formed by inserting *gèng* (even) before the modifier. The superlative is formed by inserting the word *zuì* (most).

The Best in Life

Traditionally Chinese have regarded luck, wealth, longevity, and happiness as the four blessings in life. You will find these four characters appearing on many

What time do we have to be back on board?	*Wǒmen jǐdiǎn bìxū huílai?*

Baggage Claim

Where is the (baggage claim area)?	*(Xíngli fáng) zài nǎr?*
I can't find my (suitcase).	*Wǒde (xiāngzi) zhǎo bú dào le.*
This is my (baggage claim tag).	*Zhè shì wǒde (xíngli pái).*
Are there any (carts)?	*Yǒu (xiǎo tuīchē) ma?*
Can someone help me (carry my bags)?	*Yǒu rén néng bāng wǒ (tí yīxià xíngli) ma?*
Where is the (exit)?	*(Chūkǒu) zài nǎr?*

Customs

This is mine.	*Zhè shì wǒde.*
This is not mine.	*Zhè bú shì wǒde.*
These are my (personal effects).	*Zhè shì wǒde (sīrén wùpǐn).*
I am not carrying any (precious jewelry).	*Wǒ méi dài rènhé (zhūbǎo).*
This is a (reproduction).	*Zhè shì (fùzhìpǐn).*
I'm not familiar with (these regulations).	*Wǒ bú tài shúxī (zhèxie guīdìng).*
It's in my (wife's) suitcase.	*Zài wǒ (qīzi de) xiāngzi lǐ.*
I lost it.	*Diū le.*
I gave it away.	*Sòng rén le.*
This is my (first) trip to China this year.	*Zhè shì wǒ jīnnián (dì yī) cì lái Zhōngguó.*
How much is the duty?	*Shuìkuǎn duōshao?*

我们几点必须回来?

行李房在哪儿?

我的箱子找不到了。

这是我的行李牌。

有小推车吗?

有人能帮我提一下行李吗?

出口在哪儿?

这是我的。

这不是我的。

这是我的私人物品。

我没带任何珠宝。

这是复制品。

我不太熟悉这些规定。

在我妻子的箱子里。

丢了。

送人了。

这是我今年第一次来中国。

税款多少?

decorative objects, either singly or all four together.

福 fú (luck)

祿 lù (wealth)

壽 shòu (longevity)

喜 xǐ (happiness)

Good-byes

There are many ways to say good-bye in Chinese. Here are some of the most often used ones.

Huítóu jiàn.	See you soon.
Míngtiān jiàn.	See you tomorrow.
Xià cì jiàn.	See you next time.
Yìhuìr jiàn.	See you later.
Zàijiàn.	See you again.

What You'll Hear

Dào le.	We've arrived.
Gèwèi lǚkè, qǐng zhùyì...	Attention travelers...
Nǐ qù nǎr?	Where are you going?
Qǐng náchū nǐde...	Please show your...
dēngjī pái	boarding pass
hǎiguān shēnbào dān	customs declaration
hùzhào	passport
qiānzhèng	visa
zhàoxiàngjī	camera
Shì nǐde ma?	Is this yours?

Signs

jīchǎng
Airport

hòuchēshì
**Waiting Room
(for trains, buses)**

kāiwǎng...
Leaving for...

fēiyǐnyòng shuǐ
Unpotable Water

jìnzhǐ xīyān
No Smoking

3 Local Transport

In China, local transportation is available in many forms. You can get around town by taxi, hired car, public bus, bicycle, or "bus no. 11," which simply means walking ("11" representing two legs). In Beijing, you can also ride the subway, or *dìtiě*. The most important thing to learn is how to ask for directions, and then understanding the answer.

LOCAL TRANSPORT

Getting Set

I'd like a (local) map, please.	*Qǐng gěi wǒ yì zhāng (běndì) dìtú.*
I'd like to go to (the Big Goose Pagoda).	*Wǒ xiǎng qù (Dàyàn Tǎ).*
What's the best way to get there?	*Něi tiáo lù zuìjìn?*
How far is it to (People's Park)?	*Qù (Rénmín Gōngyuán) yǒu duōyuǎn?*
Is it within walking distance?	*Zǒu de dào ma?*
How much should the fare be to (the airport)?	*Qù (jīchǎng) yào duōshao qián?*

Taking a Taxi

Where can I get a taxi?	*Nǎr néng jiàodào chūzū qìchē?*
I'd like a cab to (the Exhibition Center).	*Wǒ yào qù (Zhǎnlǎn Zhōngxīn).*
What's the fare per kilometer?	*Yì gōnglǐ duōshao qián?*
To (the Peace Hotel), please.	*Qǐng kāi dào (Hépíng Fàndiàn).*
Driver, can you take me to (this address)?	*Sījī, nǐ néng bǎ wǒ sòng dào (zhèige dìfáng) ma?*
Do you know the way there?	*Nǐ zhīdao zěnme zǒu ma?*
Please stop a moment.	*Qǐng tíng yíxià.*
Please drive (faster).	*Qǐng kāi (kuài yìdiǎn).*
Can you wait for me?	*Néng děng wǒ yíxià ma?*
I'll be back in (20) minutes.	*Wǒ (èrshí) fēnzhōng yǐhòu huílai.*

请给我一张本地地图。

我想去大雁塔。

哪条路最近?

去人民公园有多远?

走得到吗?

去机场要多少钱?

哪儿能叫到出租汽车?

我要去展览中心。

一公里多少钱?

请开到和平饭店。

司机,你能把我送到这个地方吗?

你知道怎么走吗?

请停一下。

请开快一点。

能等我一下吗?

我二十分钟以后回来。

Which Way Is North?

After you ask someone on the street for directions, listen for these key words in their answer:

北	běi	north
东	dōng	east
南	nán	south
西	xī	west
右	yòu	right
左	zuǒ	left
后	hòu	back
前	qián	front

Some common expressions used for giving directions are:

guò...	past (across)...
hónglǜdēng	the stoplight
mǎlù	the road
wàng...guǎi	turn toward...
wàng...zǒu	walk toward...
yìzhí zǒu	go straight on
zài...biān	on the...side
zài...miàn	facing the...
zǒu cuò le	wrong way

Taxi Fares

In China, every legitimate taxi is metered. Most taxis belong to state-owned taxi companies, which operate either as independent car services or in connection with travel agencies, hotels, or restaurants. Recently there has been a rise of gypsy cabs on the streets—be careful of them. When you enter a cab, make sure the driver turns on the meter. If he doesn't, say *Qǐng dǎkāi jìjiàqì* (please turn on the meter). If he still

...like to return to (the hotel).   *Ránhòu wǒ jiù huí (fàndiàn).*

This is the wrong way.   *Zǒu cuò lù le.*

Don't try to trick me.   *Bié piàn wǒ.*

Hiring a Car

I'd like to hire (a car).   *Wǒ yào bāo (yí liàng chē).*

What is the rate per (day)?   *Měi (tiān) duōshao zūjīn?*

Can I hire a car for (half a day)?   *Bāo (bàntiān) chē xíng ma?*

After how many (kilometers) will there be an extra charge?   *Chāoguò duōshao (gōnglǐ) yào lìngwài jiā qián?*

How do you charge for extra (mileage)?   *Chāoguò de (lǐchéng) zěnme shōufèi?*

Do you have a car available (now)?   *(Xiànzài) yǒu chē ma?*

I'd like to hire a car for (two) days beginning [the day after tomorrow].   *Wǒ xiǎng cóng [hòutiān] qǐ bāo (liǎng) tiān chē.*

I'll come for the car at (8:00 in the morning).   *(Zǎochén bā diǎn) wǒ yào yòng chē.*

Going by Bus

Which bus should I take to get to (the Summer Palace)?   *Qù (Yíhéyuán) zuò něi lù chē?*

Where is the nearest bus stop?   *Zuìjìn de gōnggòng qìchē zhàn zài nǎr?*

How many stops to (the zoo)?   *Qù (dòngwùyuán) yǒu jǐ zhàn?*

Does this bus go to (the Beijing Library)?   *Zhèi tàng chē qù (Běijīng Túshūguǎn) ma?*

然后我就回饭店。

走错路了。

别骗我。

我要包一辆车。

每天多少租金？

包半天车行吗？

超过多少公里要另外加钱？

超过的里程怎么收费？

现在有车吗？

我想从后天起包两天车。

早晨八点我要用车。

去颐和园坐哪路车？

最近的公共汽车站在哪儿？

去动物园有几站？

这趟车去北京图书馆吗？

refuses to turn on the meter, the best you can do is strike a hard bargain for the fare to your destination.

As of 1988, the standard taxi fare in Beijing was 80 fen per kilometer, with many cabs still charging 70 fen. Smaller taxis could occasionally be found for 60 or even 50 fen. Most taxis start their meter at four kilometers (or 3.20 yuan on a 80-fen taxi).

Bus Numbers

Buses in China are identified by their route number, so instead of saying *hào* (number) when referring to a bus, the Chinese say *lù* (route). Thus, bus no. 52 would be *wǔshí èr lù chē.*

Riding Public Buses

Public buses are the chief means of local transportation for Chinese urban residents, with fares costing from 5 fen to 25 fen depending on the distance traveled. After boarding a bus, you must make your way, if you can, to the nearest bus conductor who will be seated at a booth near one of the doors. Large buses will have more than one conductor. Tell the conductor how many tickets you want and to what destination; for example, *liǎng zhāng, Tiān'ānmén* (two tickets, Tian'anmen). He or she will tell you the price, such as *yì máo* (10 fen), and give

...[Wangfujing]. *(Yì) zhāng, [Wángfǔjīng].*

...me when to get *Dào zhàn qǐng jiào wǒ yíxià.*

...here can I transfer to bus no. (302)? *Zài nǎr néng dǎo (sān líng èr) lù chē?*

Where is the bus stop for bus no. (41)? *(Sìshí yī) lù chēzhàn zài nǎr?*

Riding the Subway

Is this a subway (entrance)? *Zhè shì dìtiě de (rùkǒu) ma?*

Does this subway go to (Chongwenmen)? *Zhèi tàng dìtiě qù (Chóngwénmén) ma?*

Where should I wait for the subway to (Beijing Railway Station)? *Qù (Běijīng Zhàn) zài nǎr děng chē?*

What is the next stop? *Xià zhàn shì nǎr?*

Make way, we want to get off. *Qǐng ràng yíxià, wǒmen yào xià chē.*

On Foot

I'm trying to find (Elephant Trunk Hill). *Wǒ zài zhǎo (Xiàngbí Shān).*

Can you direct me there? *Nǐ néng gàosù wǒ zěnme zǒu ma?*

Does this lane lead to (the main street)? *Zhèi tiáo xiǎoxiàng tōngxiàng (dàjiē) ma?*

Excuse me, could you tell me where the (CAAC office) is? *Láojià, nǐ néng gàosù wǒ (Zhōngguó Mínháng bànshìchù) zài nǎr ma?*

Is this (Chang'an Avenue)? *Zhè shì (Cháng'ān Jiē) ma?*

Is this way (north)? *Zhè shì (běi) miàn ma?*

I'm lost. *Wǒ mílù le.*

一张, 王府井。

到站请叫我一下。

在哪儿能倒 302 路车?

41 路车站在哪儿?

这是地铁的入口吗?

这趟地铁去崇文门吗?

去北京站在哪儿等车?

下站是哪儿?

请让一下, 我们要下车。

我在找象鼻山。

你能告诉我怎么走吗?

这条小巷通向大街吗?

劳驾, 你能告诉我中国民航办事处在哪儿吗?

这是长安街吗?

这是北面吗?

我迷路了。

you a ticket stub. Keep the stub in case you need to show it later. If you notice that many Chinese do not buy tickets, it's probably because they have monthly passes, known as *yuèpiào*.

When you have almost reached your stop, be sure to make your way to the door. On crowded buses it's easy to get packed in the middle of the bus and not be able to get off before the doors close and the bus moves on.

Bus Stops

Bus stops are marked by signposts along the road, or sometimes by small signs affixed to electricity poles or tree trunks. If the road is wide and an island separates it from the bicycle path, the bus stop will be on the island. The bus sign will show the route number, the name of the immediate stop, the destination toward which the bus is traveling, and the times of the first run and last run. A chart showing all the stops along the route is often included, with the immediate stop indicated by a box, an arrow, or underlining. Sometimes the sign also gives advance notice of the next stop, so be careful not to mix that up with the name of the current stop.

Some Chinese characters you will need to recognize are:

公共汽车	public bus
本站	this stop
下站	next stop
头班车	first run
首班车	first run
末班车	last run
夜班车	night bus

LOCAL TRANSPORT

| Where am I? | *Wǒ xiànzài zài nǎr?* |

Renting a Bike

I'd like to rent a bicycle.	*Wǒ xiǎng zū yí liàng zìxíngchē.*
How much is the rental for one (hour)?	*Yì (xiǎoshí) de zūjīn shì duōshao?*
How much is (the deposit)?	*(Yājīn) duōshao?*
I'd like that (blue) one.	*Wǒ yào nà liàng (lán) de.*
I'll bring it back around (4:00 in the afternoon).	*(Xiàwǔ sì diǎn) zuǒyòu wǒ lái huán chē.*
I've finished riding.	*Wǒ bú yòng chē le.*
How much do I owe?	*Duōshao qián?*
My (passport), please.	*Qǐng bǎ (hùzhào) huán wǒ.*

我现在在哪儿？

我想租一辆自行车。

一小时的租金是多少？

押金多少？

我要那辆蓝的。

下午四点左右我来还车。

我不用车了。

多少钱？

请把护照还我。

Bike Parking

China has the largest number of bicycles in the world, and that will seem quite evident if you are out on a busy street during rush hour. Parking would be a horrible problem if all the bikes were cars.

There are two types of parking spaces available for bikes. The first is in designated lots which are sectioned off and guarded by bike attendants. These parking lots charge a small fee, ranging from 2 fen during the day to 10 fen at night. The second type of space is—no kidding—almost anywhere that's convenient: outside houses, on the pavement, even on the street. However, the bike owner then runs the risk of having his bike stolen, run over, or confiscated by an earnest public-safety worker.

What You'll Hear

dǎo chē	transfer buses
Dào nǎr?	Where to?
dǎkāi piào	show your ticket
huàn chē	transfer buses
Kàn chē!	Watch out (for the bike or car)!
kuài chē	express
mǎi piào	buy a ticket
Xià ma?	Are you getting off?
Xiān xià, hòu shàng.	Let people off first, then get on.
Zhànzhù.	Halt.

Signs

chūzūqìchē zhàn

Taxi Stand

zìxíngchē xiūlǐbù

Bicycle Repair Shop

(tíng)

No Parking

chū rù qǐng xià chē

Please Get off Your Bike at the Gate

shìgù duōfā dìdiǎn

Site of Frequent Accidents

34

四 sì

4 Hotel

> **Diàntī zài nǎr?**
> Where's the elevator?

Hotels have come a long way in China, especially since the early 1980s when Western tourists began arriving in big waves. Whereas a "first-class hotel" used to mean a 1950s-style boardinghouse with simple furniture, clean bedding, and keys hung on a pegboard, these days it means a five-star hotel where you can find everything from telex machines to a health club and disco. The service people at the main desk usually know enough English to handle common requests, but the upstairs floor attendants may barely know any.

Checking In

I have already booked (one) room for [two] nights.	*Wǒ yǐjīng yùdìng le (yí) gè fángjiān zhù [liǎng] gè wǎnshang.*
Do you have a (single room) available?	*Yǒu (dān jiān) ma?*
How much is a (twin room) per night?	*(Shuāngrén fángjiān) duōshao qián?*
What is your (lowest) rate for a room?	*(Zuìpiányi) de fángjiān shì duōshao qián?*
I would like to stay (three) nights.	*Wǒ xiǎng zhù (sān) tiān.*
I would like (two) rooms next to each other.	*Wǒ yào (liǎng) gè jǐnāizhe de fángjiān.*
I would like a room facing the (garden).	*Wǒ yào yì jiān chuānghu duìzhe (huāyuán) de fángjiān.*
Does this room have a good (view)?	*Zhège fángjiān (chuāngwài de fēngjǐng) hǎo ma?*
I prefer a room on a (lower) floor.	*Wǒ xiǎng yào (dī) céng de fángjiān.*
Can an extra cot be brought in?	*Néng zài jiā yì zhāng chuáng ma?*
Do you give a discount to (foreign students)?	*Duì (liúxuéshēng) yǒu méi yǒu yōuhuì?*
Will I be able to pay by (credit card)?	*Wǒ néng yòng (xìnyòngkǎ) fùkuǎn ma?*

Checking Out

Please make up my bill.	*Qǐng bāng wǒ jiézhàng.*
My room number is (3024).	*Wǒ zhù (sān líng èr sì) fángjiān.*

我已经预定了一个
房间，住两个晚
上。

有单间吗？

双人房间多少钱？

最便宜的房间是多
少钱？

我想住三天。

我要两个紧挨着的
房间。

我要一间窗户对着
花园的房间。

这个房间窗外的风
景好吗？

我想要底层的房
间。

能再加一张床吗？

对留学生有没有优
惠？

我能用信用卡付款
吗？

请帮我结帐。

我住 3024 房间。

Local Hostels

For those of you who are traveling on a shoestring, you might choose to stay at a *lǚguǎn* (small hotel), *lǚshè* (inn), or *sùshè* (dorm or hostel). The prices there are cheap, the most you'll pay being 20 yuan for a single room to 10 yuan for a room shared with three other people. The accommodations are spartan—a cot and a TV, often black and white, no closets, and a bathroom down the hallway. Remember also that running hot water is a luxury in China, so most small establishments will not have it. When hot water is provided, the hours are usually restricted.

To request a bed in a shared room, use the phrase *Hái yǒu chuángwèi ma?* (Is there a berth available?)

Chinese Horoscope

The Chinese "horoscope" is represented by twelve animals, with one animal governing each year in a twelve-year cycle. Each animal represents one of the Twelve Earthly Branches in Chinese astrology.

Traditionally, Chinese have kept track of each other's ages by remembering what animal sign a person belongs to. For example, someone might forget how old his sister is but remember "Oh, she was born in the year of the tiger..." and figure it out from there. If you want to ask someone's age indirectly, say *Nǐ shǔ shénme?* (What do you belong to?) The twelve animals and their corresponding years in this century are listed below.

Rat	鼠	1900, 1912, 1924, 1936,
shǔ		1948, 1960, 1972, 1984

continued

HOTEL

There seems to be a mistake here.	*Zhèlǐ hǎoxiàng yǒu diǎn bú duì.*
I've paid already.	*Wǒ yǐjīng fù guò kuǎn le.*
When is check-out time?	*Shénme shíhòu tuì fáng?*
I'll be leaving tomorrow morning at (7:30).	*Wǒ míngtiān zǎochén (qī diǎn bàn) zǒu.*
Where shall I leave the key?	*Yàoshi liú zài nǎr?*

Service Inquiries

When will my (suitcases) be brought up?	*Wǒde (xíngli) shénme shíhòu néng sòng shàng lái?*
Can it be brought to my room?	*Néng sòng dào wǒde fángjiān ma?*
Where shall I pick up (the keys)?	*Wǒ dào nǎr qù ná (yàoshi)?*
Do you have another (key) for my roommate?	*Wǒde tóngwū yě néng yǒu (yì bǎ yàoshi) ma?*
Have there been any messages for me?	*Yǒu rén gěi wǒ liúhuà ma?*
Where is the (elevator)?	*(Diàntī) zài nǎr?*
When is the (bar) open?	*(Jiǔbā) shénme shíhòu kāimén?*
Do you have today's (China Daily)?	*Yǒu jīntiān de (Zhōngguó Rìbào) ma?*
Where can I find (the banquet manager)?	*Nǎr néng zhǎodào (yànhuìtīng jīnglǐ)?*
Is there some place where I can send (a telex)?	*Nǎr néng fā (diànchuán)?*
Can you help me get my (watch) repaired?	*Nǐ néng bāng wǒ xiū yíxià (biǎo) ma?*

这里好象有点不对。

我已经付过款了。

什么时候退房?

我明天早晨七点半走?

钥匙留在哪儿?

我的行李什么时候能送上来?

能送到我的房间吗?

我到哪儿去拿钥匙?

我的同屋也能有一把钥匙吗?

有人给我留话吗?

电梯在哪儿?

酒吧什么时候开门?

有今天的"中国日报"吗?

哪儿能找到宴会厅经理?

哪儿能发电传?

你能帮我修一下表吗?

Ox *niú*	牛	1901, 1913, 1925, 1937, 1949, 1961, 1973, 1985
Tiger *hǔ*	虎	1902, 1914, 1926, 1938, 1950, 1962, 1974, 1986
Rabbit *tù*	兔	1903. 1915, 1927, 1939, 1951. 1963, 1975, 1987
Dragon *lóng*	龙	1904. 1916, 1928, 1940, 1952, 1964, 1976, 1988
Snake *shé*	蛇	1905, 1917, 1929, 1941, 1953. 1965, 1977, 1989
Horse *mǎ*	马	1906, 1918, 1930, 1942, 1954, 1966, 1978, 1990
Sheep *yáng*	羊	1907, 1919, 1931, 1943, 1955, 1967, 1979, 1991
Monkey *hóu*	猴	1908, 1920, 1932, 1944, 1956, 1968, 1980, 1992
Rooster *jī*	鸡	1909, 1921, 1933, 1945, 1957, 1969, 1981, 1993
Dog *gǒu*	狗	1910, 1922, 1934, 1946, 1958, 1970, 1982, 1994
Pig *zhū*	猪	1911, 1923, 1935, 1947, 1959, 1971, 1983, 1995

Long-distance Communications

Post offices in China are the centers for long-distance telephone calls and telegrams. If you are far away from a luxury hotel and need to call home, go to a main post office. However, be prepared to wait in line to place your call or telegram. International phone calls sometimes take over an hour for the connection to be made.

HOTEL

Please wake me up tomorrow at (6:00 am). | *Qǐng zài míngtiān (zǎochén liù diǎn) jiào xǐng wǒ.*

Problems in the Room

The (toilet) doesn't work. | *(Cèsuǒ) huài le.*

The (faucet) is leaking. | *(Lóngtóu) lòushuǐ.*

Please help me open the (windows). | *Qǐng bāng wǒ dǎkāi (chuānghu).*

The door doesn't lock. | *Zhèige mén suǒ bú shàng.*

How do you turn on the (heat)? | *Zěnme kāi (nuǎnqì)?*

How do you adjust this (digital clock)? | *Zhège (diànzǐ biǎo) zěnme tiáo?*

My room is too (noisy). | *Wǒde fángjiān tài (chǎo) le.*

I'd like to change to another room. | *Wǒ xiǎng huàn yí gè fángjiān.*

Housekeeping

I need (some towels). | *Wǒ xiǎng yào (jǐ tiáo máojīn).*

May I borrow an (iron)? | *Wǒ xiǎng jiè yí gè (yùn dǒu).*

Please bring (a thermos of boiled water). | *Qǐng ná (yì píng kāishuǐ) lái.*

May I have another (blanket)? | *Néng zài gěi wǒ (yì tiáo tǎnzi) ma?*

The room needs to be cleaned. | *Zhège fángjiān gāi dǎsǎo le.*

Could you vacuum the (rug)? | *Qǐng bǎ (dìtǎn) xī gānjìng.*

Please take this away. | *Qǐng bǎ zhèige ná zǒu.*

This plug doesn't fit. | *Zhèige chātóu chā bú shàng.*

What shall I do? | *Zěnme bàn?*

请在明天早晨六点
叫醒我。

厕所坏了。

龙头漏水。

请帮我打开窗户。

这个门锁不上。

怎么开暖气?

这个电子表怎么
调?

我的房间太吵了。

我想换一个房间。

我想要几条毛巾。

我想借一个熨斗。

请拿一瓶开水来。

能再给我一条毯子
吗?

这个房间该打扫
了。

请把地毯吸干净。

请把这个拿走。

这个插头插不上。

怎么办?

Post Office Tips

Here are some helpful hints for mailing letters in China:

● Envelopes are not pre-glued on the back flap, so be sure to seal your letters by using the glue provided at the post office or in your room. Licking the back of the envelope will not work.

● The smaller denominations of postage stamps, used on domestic mail, do not have glue on the back. Again, use the glue pot.

● When you mail a letter overseas, make sure the country of destination is clearly written; if possible, include the Chinese characters for that country.

● When you mail a domestic letter in China, you can put the stamp anywhere on the envelope. In fact, Chinese often put the stamp on the back of the envelope.

English-language Publications

Several English-language magazines and one newspaper are published in China to inform foreign friends about China's viewpoints on national and international issues, its progress in the socialist construction, and general topics from sports to culture. Many hotels offer a selection of these publications free of charge. The well-known ones are:

China Daily

Founded in 1981, this is the only English-language newspaper published in China.

continued

HOTEL

Laundry

This is my laundry.	*Zhè shì wǒ yào xǐ de yīfu.*
When will I get my laundry back?	*Yīfu shénme shíhòu néng xǐ hǎo?*
Can it be done sooner?	*Néng kuài yìdiǎn ma?*
I need it (tonight).	*Wǒ (jīntiān wǎnshang) yào.*
This is to be (dry cleaned).	*Zhèi jiàn yào (gānxǐ).*
This should be (hand washed).	*Zhèi jiàn yào (yòng shǒu xǐ).*

Making a Phone Call

I'd like to make a long-distance call to (the United States).	*Wǒ xiǎng gěi (Měiguó) dǎ yí gè chángtú diànhuà.*
The number is: (123 456 7788).	*Hàomǎ shì (yī èr sān, sì wǔ liù, qī qī bā bā).*
How much does a call to (London) cost per minute?	*Gěi (Lúndūn) dǎ chángtú yì fēnzhōng duōshao qián?*
It's a collect call.	*Duìfāng fùkuǎn.*
I will pay for the call.	*Wǒ fùkuǎn.*
I'll be using my credit card.	*Wǒ yòng xìnyòngkǎ fùkuǎn.*
I'd like to call (person to person).	*Wǒ yào dǎ gè (jiàorén) diànhuà.*
I placed my call (one hour) ago.	*Wǒ (yí gè xiǎoshí) yǐqián jiù yào guò diànhuà le.*
Could you see if I can get a line soon?	*Néng bāng wǒ kuài yìdiǎn jiētōng ma?*
How much longer will I have to wait?	*Hái yào děng duōjiǔ?*
Please cancel the call I booked.	*Qǐng qǔxiāo gāngcái wǒ yào de diànhuà.*

这是我要洗的衣服。

衣服什么时候能洗好?

能快一点吗?

我今天晚上要。

这件要干洗。

这件要用手洗。

我想给美国打一个长途电话。

号码是: 123 456 7788。

给伦敦打长途一分钟多少钱?

对方付款。

我付款。

我用信用卡付款。

我要打个叫人电话。

我一个小时以前就要过电话了。

能帮我快一点接通吗?

还要等多久?

请取消刚才我要的电话。

Beijing Review

Established in 1958, this is China's only foreign-language weekly devoted to news and politics.

China Pictorial

Founded in 1950, this highly illustrated magazine reports on China's socialist construction and the life of its many nationalities.

China Reconstructs

Founded by Soong Ching Ling (Mrs. Sun Yat-sen) to promote understanding and friendship between the Chinese people and the rest of the world, this comprehensive monthly was first published in 1952.

China Sports

Established in 1957, this monthly is devoted to the sports history and achievements of Chinese athletes.

Chinese Literature

First issued in 1951, this quarterly presents the translated works of modern Chinese writers as well as art and book reviews.

Women of China

First published in 1956, this monthly reports on achievements and issues concerning women.

Chinese-language Newspapers

What do the Chinese read every day? There are over 800 registered newspapers in China, published by various organizations at the national, pro-

HOTEL

Please give me extension (800).	*Qǐng jiē (bā líng líng) fēnjī.*
Please connect me with (the main desk).	*Qǐng jiē (zǒng fúwùtái).*
The line is not clear.	*Xiànlù bù qīngchǔ.*
It was a wrong number.	*Hàomǎ cuò le.*
Could you help me make a call?	*Nǐ néng bāng wǒ dǎ yí gè diànhuà ma?*
Do I need to dial "0" first?	*Yào xiān bō "líng" ma?*

The Foreign Exchange Desk

I'd like to convert (US dollars).	*Wǒ yào duìhuàn (Měiyuán).*
I have (traveler's checks).	*Wǒ yǒu (lǚxíng zhīpiào).*
Do you accept (credit cards)?	*Néng yòng (xìnyòngkǎ) ma?*
Please give me (large) bills.	*Qǐng gěi wǒ (dà) piàozi.*
Please give me (20 yuan) in small bills and change.	*Qǐng gěi wǒ (èrshí yuán) língqián.*
May I have (a receipt)?	*Néng gěi wǒ (yì zhāng fāpiào) ma?*
Where can I get a cash advance on my credit card?	*Nǎr néng yòng xìnyòngkǎ duìhuàn xiànjīn?*
Where can I cash a (personal check)?	*Zài nǎr néng duìhuàn (zhīpiào)?*
Is this a (service fee)?	*Zhè shì (fúwù fèi) ma?*
What is the exchange rate?	*Duìhuàn lǜ shì duōshao?*

The Post Office

I'd like to mail (a letter).	*Wǒ yào jì (xìn).*

请接 800 分机。

请接总服务台。

线路不清楚。

号码错了。

你能帮我打一个电话吗？

要先拨"0"吗？

我要兑换美元。

我有旅行支票。

能用信用卡吗？

请给我大票子。

请给我二十元零钱。

能给我一张发票吗？

哪儿能用信用卡兑换现金？

在哪儿能兑换支票？

这是服务费吗？

兑换率是多少？

我要寄信。

vincial, municipal, and autonomous regional levels. The leading national newspapers are:

人民日报
Rénmín Rìbào (People's Daily)
This is the official newspaper of the CPC Central Committee. It began publication in 1947 in the North China Liberated Area.

光明日报
Guāngmíng Rìbào (Enlightenment Daily)
A newspaper mainly read by intellectuals, it began publication in 1949 as the organ of the All-China Democratic League and in 1952 became the combined organ of all the democratic parties.

经济日报
Jīngjì Rìbào (Economic Daily)
Founded in 1983, this newspaper reports on China's economic developments, reforms, products, and markets.

参考消息
Cānkǎo Xiāoxi (News Reference)
Widely read by people of all ages, this bulletin reports new developments in international politics and economy, with translations of articles from foreign presses. It originated as a pamphlet published in Yan'an in the 1930s.

体育报
Tǐyù Bào (Sports)
This is China's only nationwide sports newspaper. It is published twice a week by the State Physical Culture and Sports Commission. It began as a trial publication in 1956.

HOTEL

I'd like to buy (five) [80 fen] stamps.	*Wǒ yào mǎi (wǔ) zhāng [bā máo] de yóupiào.*
Please give me (three) [1.60 yuan] stamps.	*Qǐng mài gěi wǒ (sān) zhāng [yí kuài liù] de yóupiào.*
How much does it cost to mail a (postcard)?	*Jì (míngxìnpiàn) yào duōshao qián?*
Please send it (air mail).	*Wǒ jì (hángkōng) xìn.*
How long will it take this (package) to arrive?	*Zhèi (bāoguǒ) duōjiǔ néng dào?*
Can you write the (name of the country) in Chinese for me?	*Qǐng bāng wǒ bǎ (guó míng) xiě chéng Zhōngwén.*
Can you help me wrap this?	*Nǐ néng bāng wǒ bāo yíxià ma?*
Do you have some (string)?	*Yǒu (shéngzi) ma?*
I would like to buy some (commemorative stamps).	*Wǒ xiǎng mǎi yìxiē (jìniàn yóupiào).*
Do you have (the whole set)?	*Yǒu (quán tào de) ma?*
When is the mail collected?	*Yóudìyuán shénme shíjiān lái qǔ xìn?*

Telegrams and Telexes

I'd like to send a (telegram) to [Guangzhou].	*Wǒ xiǎng fā gè (diànbào) dào [Guǎngzhōu].*
This is (the recipient's) name and address.	*Zhè shì (duìfāng) de míngzi hé dìzhǐ.*
This is the (cable address).	*Zhè shì (diànbào guàhào).*
Shall I write the (message) here?	*(Nèiróng) shì xiě zài zhèr ma?*
Please give me a copy of the (telex).	*Qǐng gěi wǒ yí gè (diànchuán) fùběn.*

我要买五张八毛的邮票。

请卖给我三张一块六的邮票。

寄明信片要多少钱？

我寄航空信。

这包裹多久能到？

请帮我把国名写成中文。

你能帮我包一下吗？

有绳子吗？

我想买一些纪念邮票。

有全套的吗？

邮递员什么时间来取信？

我想发个电报到广州。

这是对方的名字和地址。

这是电报挂号。

内容是写在这儿吗？

请给我一个电传付本。

Tea

The most popular beverage in China is tea. Tea is said to have many curative effects, from improving eyesight and preventing tooth decay to helping reduce weight. Below are the names of the basic teas in China.

lǜchá 绿茶
Green Tea: an unfermented tea with a clear taste and dark green color. The most famous green tea is West Lake Dragon Well Tea *(xīhú lóngjǐngchá)* produced in Hangzhou. It is known for its delicate taste.

hóngchá 红茶
Black Tea: a fermented tea with a fruit fragrance and mellow taste. A famous black tea is Keemun Tea *(qíhóng)* produced in Qīmen, Anhui province. It has a sweet aftertaste.

wūlóngchá 乌龙茶
Oolong Tea: a semi-fermented tea produced in Fujian and Taiwan. A famous oolong tea is Iron Goddess of Mercy Tea *(tiěguān yīn chá)* which has a sweet aroma and concentrated taste.

huāchá 花茶
Scented Tea: a tea produced by smoke-processing tea leaves with flower petals. Jasmine Tea *(mòlìhuāchá)* is popular for its clear taste and jasmine fragrance.

zhuānchá 砖茶
Brick Tea: tea that is pressed into the shape of a brick, or other shape, after the tea leaves have been steamed. Easy to carry and store, this tea has a strong taste and can dissolve fat. It is an indispensable beverage for nationalities that eat a lot of meat.

Do you have a (telex machine)?	*Yǒu (diànchuánjī) ma?*
May I send it myself?	*Wǒ kěyǐ zìjǐ fā ma?*
I don't know how to use a (telex machine).	*Wǒ bù zhīdao zěnme yòng (diànchuánjī).*

The Barbershop

I need a (haircut).	*Wǒ yào (lǐfà).*
Please give me a (trim).	*Qǐng bāng wǒ (xiūjiǎn) yíxià.*
I'd like it rather (short).	*Wǒ yào (duǎn) diǎn.*
Please cut more (here).	*(Zhè biān) duō jiǎn diǎn.*
Please leave it long (here).	*(Zhè biān) yào cháng diǎn.*
Please do not use (conditioner).	*Qǐng bú yào yòng (hùfàsù).*
Please (blow dry) my hair.	*Qǐng bǎ tóufà (chuīgān).*
I'd like to have a (New Wave) look.	*Wǒ xiǎng yào (xīncháo) fà shì.*

有电传机吗?

我可以自己发吗?

我不知道怎么用电传机。

我要理发。

请帮我修剪一下。

我要短点。

这边多剪点。

这边要长点。

请不要用护发素。

请把头发吹干。

我想要新潮发式。

Batteries

Ran out of batteries? Don't worry, the common sizes of batteries are available in most local department stores. However, in China they are named not by alphabet but by number. Here's how to request the battery you want:

D battery (#1)	*yī hào diànchí*
C battery (#2)	*èr hào diànchí*
AA battery (#5)	*wǔ hào diànchí*
AAA battery (#7)	*qī hào diànchí*

Note: AAA batteries were just getting on the market in 1988 and may be difficult to find. The best bet is to bring your own stock.

What You'll Hear

diànhuà fèi	telephone bill
diànhuà lái le	the call has come through
fúwùtái	service desk
fúwùyuán	service attendant
Jǐ lóu?	Which floor?
lóushàng	upstairs
lóuxià	downstairs
Méi rén jiē.	No answer. (phone)
Xiān bō líng.	Dial "0" first.
zhàn xiàn	busy line (phone)

Signs

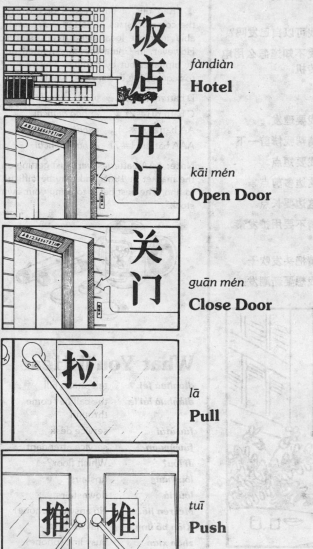

饭店
fàndiàn
Hotel

开门
kāi mén
Open Door

关门
guān mén
Close Door

拉
lā
Pull

推推
tuī
Push

Friends 5 五 wǔ

Chī le ma?
How's it going? (Eaten yet?)

In most places, you will get a warm and friendly response to your enthusiasm in speaking Chinese. A conversation can be struck and new acquaintances made with just a few simple words.

The most often used greeting, appropriate for all occasions, is *nǐhǎo* (hello). Around mealtimes, Chinese often greet each other with *Chī le ma?* (Have you eaten yet?) which is a general expression of concern for the other person. The proper reply, even if you haven't eaten for days, is *Chī le, xièxie* (I've eaten, thanks).

51

FRIENDS

Opening Lines

Hello.	*Nǐhǎo!*
How are you?	*Nǐ hǎo ma?*
(Fine), and you?	*(Hěn hǎo), nǐ ne?*
So-so.	*Hái kěyǐ.*
Not too bad.	*Bú cuò.*
Good morning.	*Zǎochén hǎo.*
Good evening.	*Wǎnshang hǎo.*
Good night.	*Wǎn'ān.*
How old are you? (to a child)	*Nǐ jǐ suì?*
How old are you? (adult)	*Nǐ jīnnián duōdà?*
I'm (twenty-five) years old.	*Wǒ (èrshí wǔ) suì.*
Where are you from?	*Nǐ shì nǎlǐ rén?*
I'm from (England).	*Wǒ shì (Yīngguó) rén.*
What do you think of (Australia)?	*Nǐ duì (Àodàlìyà) de yìnxiàng rúhé?*
This is my first trip to (China).	*Wǒ shì dìyī cì lái (Zhōngguó).*
I would like to learn some (Chinese).	*Wǒ xiǎng xué yìxiē (Zhōngwén).*

Talk About the Weather

It's a (fine) day today.	*Jīntiān tiānqì (tǐng hǎo).*
God, it's really pouring!	*Āiyā, yǔ xià de zhēn dà!*
Do you know what the forecast for (tomorrow) is?	*Nǐ zhīdao (míngtiān) de tiānqì yùbào ma?*
The weather report says it will be (cold).	*Tiānqì yùbào shuō míngtiān huì (lěng).*
Tomorrow it might (rain).	*Míngtiān kěnéng (xià yǔ).*

你好!

你好吗?

很好,你呢?

还可以。

不错。

早晨好。

晚上好。

晚安。

你几岁?

你今年多大?

我二十五岁。

你是哪里人?

我是英国人。

你对澳大利亚的印象如何?

我是第一次来中国。

我想学一些中文。

今天天气挺好。

哎呀,雨下得真大!

你知道明天的天气预报吗?

天气预报说明天会冷。

明天可能下雨。

Chinese Names

Most Chinese names consist of two or three characters, or words, with the first being the surname. If a person is called Wang Zhonghua, for example, "Wang" is his family name and "Zhonghua" his given name. In Chinese culture, to call someone by his given name is a privilege reserved for family members and close friends. Therefore, to address someone politely, you should use either the full name, such as Wang Zhonghua, or the last name plus a title, such as Wang *lǎoshī* (Teacher Wang).

In informal situations, Chinese call each other by their last names preceded by *xiǎo* (young) or *lǎo* (old). For example, if Wang Zhonghua was a young man, he would be called Xiao Wang.

If the other person is not very familiar, Chinese often use the address *tóngzhì* (comrade) or, more respectfully, *shīfu* (master worker). In crowded stores, you will even hear the salesclerk being called *shīfu*, in hopes of faster service.

In China, the titles *xiānsheng* (Mr.), *tàitai* (Mrs.), and *xiǎojiě* (Miss) are considered elitist and therefore not normally used. Chinese do address their foreign friends by these titles, however, out of courtesy.

(Psst...What'll I Call Him?)

If your friend's last name is Wang, how should you address him or her? Here are some suggestions for you to choose from, depending on Wang's age and status.

continued

FRIENDS

Talk About Family

Are you married?	*Nǐ jiéhūn le ma?*
Yes (I'm married).	*Jié le.*
No, not yet.	*Méi yǒu.*
I have (one) child.	*Wǒ yǒu (yí) gè háizi.*
Boy or girl?	*Shì nánháir háishì nǚháir?*
How old?	*Jǐ suì le?*
Do you have (brothers and sisters)?	*Nǐ yǒu (xiōngdì jiěmèi) ma?*
I have one (older sister).	*Wǒ yǒu yí gè (jiějie).*
Who are the members of your family?	*Nǐ jiā dōu yǒu shénme rén?*

Talk About Work

What do you do?	*Nǐ zuò shénme gōngzuò?*
I'm a (teacher).	*Wǒ shì (jiàoshī).*
Where do you (teach)?	*Nǐ zài nǎr (jiāoshū)?*
Are you satisfied with your (work)?	*Xǐhuan nǐde (gōngzuò) ma?*
It's not bad.	*Hái kěyǐ.*
I like (my work) very much.	*Wǒ fēicháng xǐhuan (wǒde gōngzuò).*
I'm considering (changing jobs).	*Wǒ zhèngzài kǎolǜ (diào gōngzuò) ne.*
I'm not very (satisfied).	*Bú tài (mǎnyì).*

Talk About Hobbies

What do you usually do in (your spare time)?	*Nǐ (yèyú shíjiān) gàn shénme?*

你结婚了吗?

结了。

没有。

我有一个孩子。

是男孩还是女孩?

几岁了?

你有兄弟姐妹吗?

我有一个姐姐。

你家都有什么人?

你做什么工作?

我是教师。

你在哪儿教书?

喜欢你的工作吗?

还可以。

我非常喜欢我的工作。

我正在考虑调工作呢。

不太满意。

你业余时间干什么?

elderly man	Wang *yéye*
elderly woman	Wang *nǎinai*
older person	*Lǎo* Wang

business or professional...
man	Wang *xiānsheng*
woman	Wang *nǚshì*
(Mrs.)	Wang *fūrén*
(Miss)	Wang *xiǎojiě*

young person	*Xiǎo* Wang
Driver	Wang *shīfu*
Bureau Director	Wang *júzhǎng*
School Principal	Wang *xiàozhǎng*
Manager	Wang *jīnglǐ*

Chinese Idioms

There are many four-word idioms in Chinese known as *chéngyǔ* (set phrase), which are sayings originated from folk stories. Because each *chéngyǔ* is a concise way of conveying a poignant meaning, Chinese use them often in everyday conversation. When the situation is ripe, delight your friends with these favorites.

老马识途 *Lǎo mǎ shí tú*
(old horse knows road)
Let experience take over.

熟能生巧 *Shú néng shēng qiǎo*
(mature ability brings skill)
Practice makes perfect.

亡羊补牢 *Wáng yáng bǔ láo*
(lost sheep mend fold)
Making repairs after the damage: better late than never.

掩耳盗铃 *Yǎn ěr dào líng*
(cover ears steal bell)
You're only fooling yourself.

continued

55

FRIENDS

I usually (read books).	*Wǒ jīngcháng (kàn shū).*
I like to (play soccer).	*Wǒ xǐhuan (tī zúqiú).*
What are you most (interested in)?	*Nǐ zuì (gǎnxìngqù) de shì shénme?*
I'm especially interested in (music).	*Wǒ duì (yīnyuè) tèbié gǎnxìngqù.*

Talk About Politics

Are you satisfied with China's present (economic) policy?	*Nǐ duì Zhōngguó mùqián de (jīngjì) zhèngcè mǎnyì ma?*
What areas are currently undergoing reform?	*Mùqián yǒu nǎ xiē lǐngyù zài shíxíng gǎigé?*
Do you think China's present (urban) reform is making progress?	*Nǐ rènwéi Zhōngguó mùqián de (chéngshì) gǎigé qǔdé jìnzhǎn le ma?*
Do most Chinese join the (Communist Party of China)?	*Shìfǒu dàduōshù Zhōngguó rén dōu jiārù (Zhōngguó Gòngchǎndǎng)?*
Out of every ten (young people) how many are [Party members]?	*Měi shí gè (niánqīng rén) zhōng, yǒu jǐ gè shì [Dǎng yuán]?*
Does (everyone) take part in elections?	*(Měigè rén) dōu cānjiā xuǎnjǔ ma?*
What do you think of (American) foreign policy?	*Nǐ duì (Měiguó) de wàijiāo zhèngcè zěnme kàn?*

Saying Good-bye

I'm very pleased to have met you.	*Rènshi nǐ hěn gāoxìng.*
It's been nice talking with you.	*Hěn gāoxìng néng hé nǐ jiāotán.*
Good-bye. (See you again.)	*Zàijiàn.*

我经常看书。

我喜欢踢足球。

你最感兴趣的是什么?

我对音乐特别感兴趣。

你对中国目前的经济政策满意吗?

目前有哪些领域在实行改革?

你认为中国目前的城市改革取得进展了吗?

是否大多数中国人都加入中国共产党?

每十个年青人中有几个是党员?

每个人都参加选举吗?

你对美国的外交政策怎么看?

认识你很高兴。

很高兴能和你交谈。

再见。

一箭双雕   *Yi jiàn shuāng diāo*
(one arrow two hawks)
Killing two birds with one stone.

Seeing Off a Friend

It is an age-old custom in China to see friends to the gate when they leave one's home. Many classic poems, in fact, describe the sadness of that moment of final parting. Here are some phrases that are still used every time a guest leaves.

Wǒ sòng sòng nǐ.	Let me see you off.
Bú sòng, bú sòng.	No, no, it's not necessary.
Méi guānxi, méi guānxi.	It's nothing, don't worry.
Qǐng liúbù.	Please don't trouble —this is far enough.
Shù bù yuǎn sòng.	All right, pardon my not seeing you out farther.

What You'll Hear

bù hǎoyìsi	feel embarrassed
Bú jiàn bú sàn.	I'll be there. Don't leave without me.
Chōuyān ma?	Do you smoke?
gòuqiàng	not likely
Hǎo jiǔ bú jiàn.	Long time no see.
huānyíng	welcome
Jiùshì!	Precisely!
Jiù zhèyàng ba.	That's settled, then.
Zāo gāo le.	It's a disaster.
Zěnme huí shì(r)?	What happened here?

Signs

讲文明 *jiǎng wénmíng*
Be Civilized

讲礼貌 *jiǎng lǐmào*
Be Polite

讲卫生 *jiǎng wèishēng*
Be Cleanly

讲纪律 *jiǎng jìlǜ*
Be Orderly

讲道德 *jiǎng dàodé*
Be Moral

Food **6** 六
liù

Wèidao hǎo jí le!
Delicious!

Hungry? Need a quick pickup? Dying for a hamburger?
Not to worry—China offers some of the best food in the
world, if only you know where to find it and how to ask
for it. You can find food on the train, in the hotel, at a
snack stall, and, of course, in a restaurant. Whether
you're buying a bowl of noodles or ordering a twenty-
course banquet, the phrases in this chapter will help
you make clear what you want.

FOOD

Eating on the Run

I'm thirsty.	*Wǒ kě le.*
I'm hungry.	*Wǒ è le.*
I'm starving.	*Wǒ è sǐ le.*
Where can I get something to eat?	*Nǎr yǒu mài chī de?*
Where can I buy a (cold drink)?	**Nǎr mài (lěngyǐn)?**
(Two) bottles of [beer], please.	*Qǐng lái (liǎng) píng [pijiǔ].*
I'd like a cup of (coffee).	*Wǒ yào yì bēi (kāfēi).*
Please give me a bowl of (noodles).	*Qǐng lái yì wǎn (miàntiáo).*
How much is this?	*Zhège dūoshao qián?*
Give me (one), please.	*Qǐng gěi wǒ (yi) gè.*
I don't have any (grain coupons).	*Wǒ méi yǒu (liáng piào).*
Do I need to return the (bottle)?	*Yào tuì (píng) ma?*
I'm leaving the (bowl) here.	*Wǒ bǎ (wǎn) fàng zài zhèr.*
Do I get back a (deposit)?	**Yǒu (yājīn) ma?**

Finding a Place to Eat

Where is there a good (restaurant)?	*Nǎr yǒu hǎo yìdiǎn de (fànguǎn)?*
Is it (expensive)?	*(Guì) bú (guì)?*
I would like to go to a (Sichuan) restaurant.	*Wǒ xiǎng qù yì jiā (Sìchuān) cāntīng.*
We would like a simple meal.	*Wǒmen xiǎng chī jiǎndān yìdiǎn.*

What's for Breakfast?

我渴了。

我饿了。

我饿死了。

哪儿有卖吃的?

哪儿卖冷饮?

请来两瓶啤酒。

我要一杯咖啡。

请来一碗面条。

这个多少钱?

请给我一个。

我没有粮票。

要退瓶吗?

我把碗放在这儿。

有押金吗?

哪儿有好一点的饭馆?

贵不贵?

我想去一家四川餐厅。

我们想吃简单一点。

Chinese rarely have bacon and eggs for breakfast. Instead, they have a bowl of hot rice congee with a few pickled vegetables or other side dishes. On the run, instead of a doughnut and coffee, Chinese have *yóutiáo* (fried cruller) and *dòujiāng* (soybean milk). If you'd like to try breakfast Chinese-style, ask a local friend where to find these favorite items:

包子	*bāozi* steamed dumpling
大米粥	*dàmǐzhōu* rice congee
豆浆	*dòujiāng* soybean milk
豆沙包	*dòushābāo* steamed bean-paste dumpling
煎饼	*jiānbǐng* crepe (with cruller)
泡菜	*pàocài* pickled vegetables
肉松	*ròusōng* shredded dried meat
烧饼	*shāobǐng* sesame seed biscuit
汤面	*tāng miàn* soup noodles
咸鸭蛋	*xián yādàn* salted duck egg
油条	*yóutiáo* fried cruller
榨菜	*zhàcài* hot pickled mustard
炸糕	*zhágāo* fried sticky-rice cake

FOOD

I'm dying for a (Western meal).

Wŏ fēicháng xiăng chī (Xīcān).

There's a (fast-food place) nearby.

Fùjìn yŏu yì jiā (kuàicān diàn).

Let's go.

Zŏu ba.

Making Reservations

I'd like to make a reservation for (Tuesday) night.

Wŏ xiăng yùdìng (xīngqī èr) wănshang de fàn.

We'll arrive at (7:30).

Wŏmen (qī diăn bàn) lái.

There will be (four) people.

(Sì) gè rén.

I'd like to pay (forty) yuan per person.

Mĕi rén (sìshi) yuán.

Will you be able to accommodate us?

Nĭmen néng jiēdài ma?

What time would be better?

Shénme shíjiān jiào hăo?

How much is it per person?

Mĕi rén duōshao qián?

Are beverages included?

Bāokuò yĭnliào ma?

Is there anything (cheaper)?

Yŏu (piányi yìdiăn) de ma?

Okay, that'll do.

Hăo, jiù zhèyàng.

See you (Tuesday).

(Xīngqī èr) jiàn.

Getting a Table

A party of (three).

Wŏmen (sān) gè rén.

A table for (two), please.

(Liăng) gè rén zuò năr?

There's a draft here.

Zhèr yŏu fēng.

Could we switch to another table?

Néng huàn gè zhuōzi ma?

May we sit over there?

Néng zuò zài nàr ma?

我非常想吃西餐。

附近有一家快餐店。

走吧！

我想预定星期二晚上的饭。

我们七点半来。

四个人。

每人四十元。

你们能接待吗？

什么时间较好？

每人多少钱？

包括饮料吗？

有便宜一点的吗？

好，就这样。

星期二见。

我们三个人。

两个人坐哪儿？

这儿有风。

能换个桌子吗？

能坐在那儿吗？

What's for Dinner?

You've finally found a place to eat. You're seated at the table, and the waiter has handed you the menu. Now what? If you are puzzled by the menu at hand, try pointing to some of the choices below and asking *Yǒu méi yǒu zhèige?* (Do you have this?) The items here are standard dishes available at most restaurants.

香酥鸡	*xiāngsūjī*	crispy fried chicken
宫保鸡丁	*gōngbǎo jīdīng*	hot spicy chicken with peanuts
糖醋鱼	*tángcù yú*	sweet-and-sour fish
红烧鱼	*hóngshāo yú*	braised fish in brown sauce
木须肉	*mùxu ròu*	mushu pork
鱼香肉丝	*yúxiāng ròusī*	pork in hot garlic sauce
葱头炒牛肉	*cōngtóu chǎo niúròu*	beef with onions
麻婆豆付	*mápó dòufu*	hot spicy beancurd
砂锅豆付	*shāguō dòufu*	beancurd casserole
香菇冬笋	*xiānggū dōngsǔn*	black mushrooms and bamboo
蘑菇菜心	*mógu càixīn*	Chinese cabbage with mushrooms
炒豆芽	*chǎo dòuyá*	sauteed bean sprouts
酸辣汤	*suānlà tāng*	hot-and-sour soup

continued

Ordering

Waiter!	*Fúwùyuán!*
Miss!	*Xiǎojiě!*
The menu, please.	*Qǐng gěi wǒmen càidān.*
What is the house specialty?	*Zhèr yǒu shénme míng cài?*
What regional cuisine do you serve here?	*Zhèr yǒu shénme fēngwèi cài?*
Do you have (Peking Duck)?	*You (kǎoyā) ma?*
Can you recommend some dishes?	*Nǐ néng tuījiàn yìxiē cài ma?*
I like (chicken).	*Wǒ xǐhuan chī (jī).*
My favorite food is (shrimp).	*Wǒ zuì ài chī (xiā).*
I don't like (mushrooms).	*Wǒ bù xǐhuan (mógu).*
I don't eat (pork).	*Wǒ bù chī (zhūròu).*
I'm vegetarian.	*Wǒ zhǐ chī sùcài.*
I'm allergic to (seafood).	*Wǒ chī (hǎixiān) huì guòmǐn.*
Please order more (vegetables).	*Qǐng duō lái jǐ pán (shūcài).*
What (soups) do you have?	*Yǒu shénme (tāng)?*
Is the (fish) fresh?	*(Yú) xīnxiān ma?*
Please leave out the (MSG).	*Qǐng bú yào fàng (wèijīng).*
Please don't make it too (spicy).	*Bú yào tài (là).*
May I order now?	*Kěyǐ diǎncài le ma?*
I'll have...	*Wǒ yào...*
one (homestyle beancurd)	*yí gè (jiācháng dòufu)*
(two) bowls of rice	*(liǎng) wǎn mǐfàn*
a pot of (jasmine) tea	*yì hú (mòlihuā) chá*

米饭	*mǐfàn*
	rice
馒头	*mántou*
	steamed roll

服务员!

小姐!

请给我们菜单。

这儿有什么名菜?

这儿有什么风味菜?

有烤鸭吗?

你能推荐一些菜吗?

我喜欢吃鸡。

我最爱吃虾。

我不喜欢蘑菇。

我不吃猪肉。

我只吃素菜。

我吃海鲜会过敏。

请多来几盘蔬菜。

有什么汤?

鱼新鲜吗?

请不要放味精。

不要太辣。

可以点菜了吗?

我要⋯⋯

　　一个家常豆腐
　　两碗米饭
　　一壶茉莉花茶

Local Snacks

As you travel throughout China, you will have the chance to sample many local snacks. Below are some of the most popular snacks in four major cities.

Beijing

冰糖葫芦	*bīngtáng húlu*
	candied haws on a stick
涮羊肉	*shuànyángròu*
	Mongolian hot pot
豌豆黄	*wāndòuhuáng*
	pea-flour cake
杏仁茶	*xìngrénchá*
	almond-flour tea
羊肉串	*yángròuchuàn*
	mutton shish kebab

Shanghai

豆沙包	*dòushābāo*
	sweet bean-paste dumplings
馄饨	*húndùn*
	wontons
小笼包	*xiǎolóngbāo*
	small steamed dumplings
芝麻汤团	*zhīma tāngtuán*
	sesame sweet-rice dumplings in soup

Xi'an

饸饹	*héle*
	buckwheat spaghetti
面皮	*miànpí*
	flat noodles made of

continued

FOOD

During the Meal

That's not what I ordered.
Zhè bú shì wǒ diǎn de cài.

I asked for (curried chicken).
Wǒ yào de shì (gālí jī).

This is too (salty).
Zhèige tài (xián) le.

This is not (fresh).
Zhèige bù (xīnxiān).

The food is (cold).
Cai (liáng) le.

What (meat) is this?
Zhè shì shénme (ròu)?

May we have some (forks)?
Néng gěi wǒmen jǐgè (chāzi) ma?

Do you have any (hot sauce)?
Yǒu (làjiàng) ma?

We need some (napkins).
Wǒmen yào (cānjīnzhǐ).

This dish is (excellent).
Zhège cài (hǎo chī ji le).

Can you write down the (name of the dish) for me?
Nǐ néng bāng wǒ xiě xià (cài míng) ma?

Ending the Meal

We have finished.
Chī wán le.

Check, please.
Jiézhàng ba.

That was a (very good) meal.
Zhè dùn fàn chī de (hěn hǎo).

We enjoyed it.
Wǒmen hěn mǎnyì.

66

这不是我点的菜。

我要的是咖喱鸡。

这个太咸了。

这个不新鲜。

菜凉了。

这是什么肉?

能给我们几个叉子吗?

有辣酱吗?

我们要餐巾纸。

这个菜好吃极了。

你能帮我写下菜名吗?

吃完了。

结帐吧。

这顿饭吃得很好。

我们很满意。

steamed refined wheat dough, served with sauces and seasonings

| 柿子饼 | shìzibǐng |
| | fried persimmon cake |

| 羊肉泡馍 | yángròu pàomó |
| | crumbled unleavened bread soaked in lamb stew |

Guangzhou

| 春卷 | chūnjuǎn (chun kuen)* |
| | spring roll |

| 烧麦 | shāomai (siu mai) |
| | steamed pork dumpling |

| 虾饺 | xiājiǎo (ha kaau) |
| | shrimp dumplings |

鲜荷叶饭	xiān héyè fàn
	(sin haw mai faan)
	rice wrapped in fresh lotus leaf

| 炸虾球 | zháxiāqiú (cha ha k'ow) |
| | fried shrimp balls |

* Cantonese pronunciations are in parentheses.

What You'll Hear

Gānbēi!	Cheers! Bottoms up.
Hái yào shénme?	Would you like anything else?
Jǐ wèi?	How many people?
Nǐmen xiǎng hē shénme?	What would you like to drink?
Nǐmen yùdìng le ma?	Do you have a reservation?
Qǐng jiézhàng.	Please pay the bill.
Yào mǐfàn ma?	Do you want rice?
Zhù nǐ jiànkāng!	To your health!

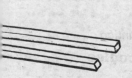

Signs

cāntīng
Dining Hall, Restaurant

lěngyǐn rèyǐn
Cold and Hot Drinks

yān jiǔ shípǐn
Cigarettes, Liquor, Foodstuffs

shuǐjiǎo
Boiled Dumplings

miàntiáo
Noodles

Sightseeing 7 七 qī

Tài bàng le!
Wow! Too much!

China abounds with scenic, historic, and cultural attractions, as well as factories and schools to visit. You will have questions to ask and comments to make at each site. Whether seeking facts or simply asking someone to move aside for a photograph, it will be invaluable to know a few words of Chinese.

Planning Your Excursion

Can you tell me where the (China International Travel Service) is?	*Nǐ néng gàosù wǒ (Zhōngguó Guójì Lǚxíng Shè) zài nǎr ma?*
I need an English-speaking (guide).	*Wǒ xūyào yí gè Yīngyǔ (dǎoyóu).*
What will be the fee per (hour)?	*Měi (xiǎoshí) duōshao qián?*
Can you arrange a trip to (Xi'an)?	*Néng ānpái dào (Xī'ān) lǚxíng ma?*
Can you recommend a (sightseeing tour)?	*Néng tuījiàn yì tiáo (guānguāng lùxiàn) ma?*
I want to see some (scenic spots).	*Wǒ xiǎng kàn yìxiē (fēngjǐng diǎn).*
I would like to visit a (factory).	*Wǒ xiǎng cānguān yí gè (gōngchǎng).*
Do you have a (local) map?	*Yǒu (dāngdì) dìtú ma?*
What are the (places of interest) in this city?	*Zhèige chéngshì yǒu shénme (kě kàn de dìfang)?*
What is the itinerary?	*Lǚyóu rìchéng shì zěnme ānpái de?*
Are we going by (bus)?	*Shì zuò (qìchē) qù ma?*
How long will the ride be?	*Zuò chē yào duōjiǔ?*
When do we set out?	*Shénme shíhou chūfā?*

At the Site

What (park) is this?	*Zhè shì shénme (gōngyuán)?*
When was this (palace) built?	*Zhèige (gōngdiàn) shì shénme shíhou jiàn de?*

你能告诉我中国国际旅行社在哪儿吗？

我需要一个英语导游。

每小时多少钱？

能安排到西安旅行吗？

能推荐一条观光路线吗？

我想看一些风景点。

我想参观一个工厂。

有当地地图吗？

这个城市有什么可看的地方？

旅游日程是怎么安排的？

是坐汽车去吗？

坐车要多久？

什么时候出发？

这是什么公园？

这个宫殿是什么时候建的？

Symbols

Chinese art is full of symbolic images —you will often see dragons, or peaches, or plum blossoms on paintings, architecture, textiles, and decorative objects. What do these motifs stand for? Below are some of the traditional symbols and their meanings.

bat: luck

chrysanthemum: nobility, purity

crane: longevity

dragon: the emperor; China

lion: power, dignity

lotus: purity, continuity

mandarin ducks: marital harmony

peach: long life, immortality

peony: wealth, honor

phoenix: the empress

pine tree: longevity

plum blossom: transience, delicacy

tiger: guardian against evil

tortoise: longevity

Flowers

China's vast territory extends across the frigid, temperate, and tropical zones, making it possible for a great variety of plant species. Below are the names of some common flowers in China. Use this list when asking a local friend *Zhè shì shénme huā*? (What flower is this?)

茶花	*cháhuā*	camelia
杜鹃花	*dùjuānhuā*	azalea
凤仙花	*fèngxiānhuā*	touch-me-not
桂花	*guìhuā*	cassia

continued

SIGHTSEEING

How large is (Tian'anmen Square)?	*(Tiān'ānmén Guǎngchǎng) duōdà?*
How high is this (pagoda)?	*Zhèige (tǎ) duōgāo?*
What does this (lion) symbolize?	*Zhèige (shīzi) dàibiǎo shénme?*
Whom does this picture portray?	*Zhèi zhāng huà huà de shì shéi?*
What other (temples) can I visit?	*Hái yǒu shénme (sìmiào) kě kàn?*
How long will we stay here?	*Wǒmen yào zài zhèr dāi duōjiǔ?*
I want to buy some (souvenirs).	*Wǒ xiǎng mǎi yìxiē (jìniàn pǐn).*

At the Zoo

I would like to see the (giant pandas).	*Wǒ xiǎng kàn (dàxióngmāo).*
Where is its habitat?	*Tā zhù zài shénme dìfang?*
What does (it) eat?	*(Tā) chī shénme?*
How many cubs does the (panda) have in one brood?	*(Xióngmāo) yì tāi shēng jǐge?*
How old is this (panda)?	*Zhèige (xióngmāo) duōdà le?*

At the Factory

May I ask a few questions?	*Wǒ kěyǐ wèn jǐgè wèntí ma?*
What are your products?	*Nǐmen yǒu shénme chǎnpǐn?*
How many (workers) do you have?	*Nǐmen yǒu duōshao (gōngrén)?*
How long does it take to complete (one carpet)?	*Zuò (yí kuài dìtǎn) yào duōcháng shíjiān?*

天安门广场多大?

这个塔多高?

这个狮子代表什么?

这张画画的是谁?

还有什么寺庙可看?

我们要在这儿呆多久?

我想买一些纪念品。

我想看大熊猫。

它住在什么地方?

它吃什么?

熊猫一胎生几个?

这个熊猫多大了?

我可以问几个问题吗?

你们有什么产品?

你们有多少工人?

做一块地毯要多长时间?

荷花	héhuā	lotus
鸡冠花	jīguānhuā	cock's comb
夹竹桃	jiāzhútáo	oleander
腊梅	làméi	allspice
兰花	lánhuā	orchid
茉莉	mòli	jasmine
牡丹	mǔdan	tree peony
蔷薇	qiángwēi	hedge rose
秋海棠	qiūhǎitáng	begonia
芍药	sháoyao	peony
水浮莲	shuǐfúlián	water lily
水仙	shuǐxiān	narcissus
绣球	xiùqiú	geranium
月季	yuèjì	Chinese rose

Trees

China observes arbor day on March 12, when young trees are planted all across the country. In southern towns, shade trees often line both sides of the streets, providing refuge from the summer heat. When identifying the trees you see, refer to the list below.

白果树	báiguǒshù	gingko
白杨树	báiyángshù	aspen
柏树	bǎishù	cypress
松树	sōngshù	pine
丁香树	dīngxiāngshù	lilac
核桃树	hétaoshù	walnut
槐树	huáishù	locust
柳树	liǔshù	willow
榕树	róngshù	banyan
桑树	sāngshù	mulberry
石榴树	shíliushù	pomegranate
柿子树	shìzishù	persimmon

continued

SIGHTSEEING

How long did you train for this job?	*Nǐ xué guò duōjiǔ?*
Do you have a (labor union)?	*Nǐmen yǒu (gōnghuì) ma?*
Do you use a (bonus system)?	*Nǐmen yǒu (jiǎngjīn zhìdù) ma?*
What is the monthly salary of a (worker)?	*(Gōngrén) měi yuè gōngzī duōshao?*
What are your working hours?	*Nǐmen měi tiān jǐdiǎn shàngxià bān?*
What is your work quota per (day)?	*Měi (tiān) de gōngzuò liàng shì duōshao?*

Taking a Photo

Can I take a picture here?	*Néng zài zhèr zhàoxiàng ma?*
Do you mind if I photograph you?	*Kěyǐ gěi nǐ zhào zhāng xiàng ma?*
Would you take a picture for me, please?	*Nǐ néng tì wǒ zhào zhāng xiàng ma?*
Everything is set.	*Dōu tiáo hǎo le.*
Just press the button.	*Zhǐ yào àn kuàimén jiù xíng le.*
Excuse me, please move aside.	*Duìbuqǐ, qǐng ràng yíxià.*
We want to take a picture here.	*Wǒmen xiǎng zài zhèr zhào zhāng xiàng.*
Please give me your address.	*Qǐng gěi wǒ nǐde dìzhǐ.*
I'll send you (the photos) later.	*Yǐhòu wǒ bǎ (zhàopiàn) gěi nǐ jì qù.*

你学过多久?

你们有工会吗?

你们有奖金制度吗?

工人每月工资多少?

你们每天几点上下班?

每天的工作量是多少?

能在这儿照相吗?

可以给你照张相吗?

你能替我照张相吗?

都调好了。

只要按快门就行了。

对不起,请让一下。

我们想在这儿照张相。

请给我你的地址。

以后我把照片给你寄去。

桃树	*táoshù*	peach
梧桐树	*wútóngshù*	Chinese parasol
柚子树	*yòuzishù*	pomelo
榆树	*yúshù*	elm
樟树	*zhāngshù*	camphor

Zoo Animals

When you visit zoos in China, you will see a few animals that are not often found in Western zoos. The all-time favorite, of course, is the giant panda. Here are the names of some animals particular to China.

大熊猫	*dàxióngmāo*	giant panda
丹顶鹤	*dāndǐnghè*	red-crowned crane
金丝猴	*jīnsīhóu*	golden-haired monkey
滩羊	*tānyáng*	argali sheep
小熊猫	*xiǎo-xióngmāo*	lesser panda

What You'll Hear

Dōu dào le.	We're all here.
Guānmén le.	It's closed.
Jīntiān xiūxi.	Today is the day off.
lǎowài	foreigner (slang)
ménpiào	admission ticket
míngxìnpiàn	postcard
wàibīn	foreign guest
wàiguórén	foreigner
Xiǎoxīn!	Careful!
Yánjìn pāizhào.	Photography prohibited.

Signs

huānyíng
Welcome

shòu piào chù
Ticket Office

ménpiào: 2 jiǎo
Admission: 20 fen

bù zhǔn suídì tùtán
No Spitting

yóukè zhǐ bù
Visitors Keep Out

八 bā 8 Shopping

Duōshao qián?
How much?

Shopping in China outside the Friendship Stores and other shops catering to foreign tourists is like treasure-hunting in a jungle. The hunt will be much easier if you can describe what you want and, more importantly, get the attention of the salesclerk.

In the many free markets that have sprung up all over China, the key phrase after *Duōshao qián?* (How much?) is *Tài guì le* (too expensive). In nongovernment stores, especially high-priced souvenir shops, you can try *Néng piányi yìdiǎn ma?* (Can the price be lowered?) Then be prepared to bargain!

77

SHOPPING

Scouting the Market

Where is the nearest (arts and crafts store)?	*Zuìjìn de (gōngyì měishù shāngdiàn) zài nǎr?*
Can you recommend a (department store)?	*Nǐ néng jièshào yí gè (bǎihuò shāngdiàn) ma?*
I would like to buy some (silk fabric).	*Wǒ xiǎng mǎi diǎn (sīchóu).*
Can you accompany me to the (free market)?	*Nǐ néng péi wǒ qù (zìyóu shìchǎng) ma?*
When does it open?	*Shénme shíhou kāimén?*

Making the Find

Comrade!	*Tóngzhì!*
Miss!	*Xiǎojiě!*
Can you help me?	*Qǐng bāng yíxià máng.*
I'd like to take a look at this (jacket).	*Wǒ xiǎng kàn yíxià zhèi jiàn (jiākè shān).*
Do you have any (others)?	*Yǒu (qítā) de ma?*
I'm looking for (cloisonne vases).	*Wǒ xiǎng mǎi (jǐngtàilán huāpíng).*
This has a (flaw).	*Zhèige yǒu (máobing).*
Please show me (that one).	*Qǐng gěi wǒ (nèige) kànkan.*
Is this (handmade)?	*Zhè shì (shǒugōng zuò de) ma?*
What kind of fabric is this?	*Zhè shì shénme liàozi de?*
Where is it made?	*Nǎr chǎn de?*
How much is it?	*Duōshao qián?*
Can you bring the price down?	*Néng piányi diǎn ma?*

Cashier's Booth

Many local stores have a cashier's booth where you must pay for your purchase before picking it up at the sales counter. When you have decided what to buy, the salesclerk at the counter will write out a bill and give you two copies. Take those copies to the cashier's booth, pay the amount shown, and return with a stamped copy of the bill as your receipt. When you hand the receipt to the salesclerk, he or she will give you your goods.

Special Items

The true shopper cannot be deterred, language barrier or not. If you wish to buy a few special Chinese items but have difficulty telling the store clerk what you want, try pointing to the list below. (Refer to the dictionary section for pronunciations.)

最近的工艺美术商店在哪儿?

你能介绍一个百货商店吗?

我想买点丝绸。

你能陪我去自由市场吗?

什么时候开门?

同志!

小姐!

请帮一下忙。

我想看一下这件夹克衫。

有其他的吗?

我想买景泰兰花瓶。

这个有毛病。

请给我那个看看。

这是手工做的吗?

这是什么料子的?

哪儿产的?

多少钱?

能便宜点吗?

竹编	bambooware (woven)
蜡染	batik
织锦	brocade
中山装	cadre's jacket
毛笔	calligraphy brush
地毯	carpet
开士米毛衣	cashmere sweater
旗袍	cheongsam (gown)
图章	chop (seal)
泥人	clay figurine
景泰蓝	cloisonne
棉衣	cotton-padded jacket
棉鞋	cotton-padded shoes
双面绣	double-sided embroidery
折扇	folding fan

continued

Closing the Deal

Okay, I'll take it.	*Hǎo, jiù yào tā.*
It's too expensive.	*Tài guì le.*
I don't want it.	*Wǒ bú yào.*
Could you wrap it for me, please?	*Qǐng bāo yíxià, hǎo ma?*
Do you have a (box) for it?	*Yǒu (hézi) ma?*
Please give me (a receipt).	*Qǐng gěi wǒ (fāpiào).*

Art and Antiques

Is this an (original)?	*Zhè shì (yuánzuò) ma?*
Is the (calligrapher) still living?	*Zhèige (shūfǎjiā) hái huózhe ma?*
Would you write down the artist's (brief background)?	*Néng bǎ zhèige yìshùjiā de (jiǎndān qíngkuàng) xiě gěi wǒ ma?*
Do you sell (reproductions)?	*Zhèr mài (fùzhìpǐn) ma?*
When was this made?	*Zhè shì shénme niándài de?*
What dynasty does it date from?	*Tā shì nǎge cháodài de?*
I must have one with a red wax seal on it.	*Wǒ yào yí gè dǎguò huǒqī yìn de.*
I won't be able to take this (out of the country).	*Zhèige wǒ bù néng dài (chū jìng).*

Books

I'm looking for a (good) English-Chinese dictionary.	*Wǒ xiǎng mǎi yì běn (hǎo) de Yīng-Hàn zìdiǎn.*
Where are the (children's) books?	*(Értóng) shū zài nǎr?*

好，就要它。

太贵了。

我不要。

请包一下好吗？

有盒子吗？

请给我发票。

这是原作吗？

这个书法家还活着吗？

能把这个艺术家的简单情况写给我吗？

这儿卖复制品吗？

这是什么年代的？

它是哪个朝代的？

我要一个打过火漆印的。

这个我不能带出境。

我想买一本好的英汉字典。

儿童书在哪儿？

皮帽子	fur hat
砚台	ink slab
墨	ink stick
铁花	iron openwork
玉雕	jade carving
漆器	lacquerware
瓷器	porcelain
军帽	Mao cap
军便服	Mao jacket
鼻烟壶	miniature bottle painting
微雕	miniature carving
剪纸	papercut
珍珠霜	pearl cream
印泥	red paste for seals
宣纸	rice paper
檀香扇	sandalwood fan
皮影	shadow puppet
贝雕画	shell mosaic
丝绸	silk fabric
丝绸睡袍	silk robe
拓片	stone rubbings
壁毯	tapestry
清凉油	tiger balm
鸭舌帽	worker's cap

Buying Jade

The main factors that go into the price of a piece of jade are the material used, the carving skill, and the color. In the Chinese jade industry, the materials are grouped into three categories. They are:

fěicuì 翡翠

Chrysolite. The most valuable jade, its color appears green but on close inspection can be seen to have both white and green elements. *continued*

SHOPPING

I'm looking for a book about Chinese (youth).

Wǒ xiǎng mǎi yì běn guānyú Zhōngguó (qīngnián) de shū.

I'm looking for works by (Lu Xun).

Wǒ xiǎng mǎi (Lǔ Xùn) de zuòpǐn.

Do you have (this book)?

Yǒu (zhè běn shū) ma?

Clothing

Can I try it on?

Néng shì yíxià ma?

Do you have a (large)?

Yǒu (dà hào) de ma?

Is there a (mirror)?

Yǒu (jìngzi) ma?

Please show me a (smaller) one.

Yǒu (xiǎo yìdiǎn) de ma?

I'd like something (brighter).

Wǒ xǐhuan (yánsè xiānyàn yìdiǎn) de.

I wear size (42).

Wǒ chuān (sìshí èr) hào.

Film

I'd like (two) rolls of [color-print film].
   (36) exposures
   (135) mm
   (100) ASA

Wǒ xiǎng mǎi (liǎng) gè [cǎijuǎn].
   (sānshí liù) zhāng de
   (yāo sān wǔ) de
   (yìbǎi) dù de

I'd like (Kodak) film.

Wǒ xiǎng yào (Kēdá) jiāojuǎn.

Where can I have (slides) processed?

Nǎr néng chōng (fǎnzhuǎn piàn)?

I'd like to have this film (developed).

Wǒ yào (chōng) jiāojuǎn.

Please do not (make prints).

Bú yào (kuòyìn).

I'd like to (order reprints).

Wǒ xiǎng (jiāyìn jǐ zhāng).

Please print (one) of this.

Zhèige qǐng yìn (yì) zhāng.

我想买一本关于中国青年的书。

我想买鲁迅的作品。

有这本书吗?

能试一下吗?

有大号的吗?

有镜子吗?

有小一点的吗?

我喜欢颜色鲜艳一点的。

我穿 42 号。

我想买两个彩卷。

  36 张的
  135 的
  100 度的

我想要柯达胶卷。

哪儿能冲反转片?

我要冲胶卷。

不要扩印。

我想加印几张。

这个请印一张。

mănăo 玛瑙
Agate. The second most valuable, it is semi-transparent. Most agate pieces are red, white, or the two colors mixed.

xiù yù 岫玉 (and others)
Manchurian jasper. A serpentine, this stone is used in the less expensive jade pieces. This third category also includes other materials, such as crystals.

How to Bargain

You're at a free market. You see the perfect cotton vest to bring home for a souvenir. But the vendor is sharp—you know he's out to scalp you. How do you bring the price down? It takes creative thinking and determination. (B is the buyer, and V is the vendor).

B: *Zhèi jiàn mián bèixīn duōshao qián?*
How much is this cotton vest?

V: *Shí kuài qián.*
Ten yuan.

B: *Shénme? Kāi wánxiào. Shí kuài qián! Tài guì le! Wŭ kuài zĕnmeyàng?*
What? You've got to be kidding. Ten yuan! Too much! How's five yuan?

V: *Bù xíng, bù xíng. Gĕi jiŭ kuài qián ba.*
No way, no way. Give me nine, then.

B: *Jiŭ kuài! Bú yào. Nĭ zhèi jiàn bèixīn zhìliàng bù hăo. Zuìduō gĕi nĭ qī kuài.*
Nine yuan! I don't want it. The quality of this vest is not very good. The most I'll offer is seven yuan.

V: *Qī kuài! Zài jiā yìdiăn ba.*
Seven yuan! Come on, raise it a little.

B: *Hăo le, hăo le. Gĕi nĭ qī kuài wŭ ba.*
Okay, okay. I'll give you seven and a half.

continued

SHOPPING

Please use (Fuji) paper.

Qĭng yòng (Fùshì) xiàngzhĭ.

When can I pick them up?

Shénme shíhou qŭ?

Can it be done earlier?

Néng zăo yìdiăn ma?

I'll be leaving town in (two) days.

(Liăng) tiān hòu wŏ jiù zŏu le.

Returns and Repairs

I'd like to return this.

Wŏ xiăng tuì huò.

It doesn't work.

Tā huài le.

Do you fix (cameras)?

Nĭmen xiū (zhàoxiàngjī) ma?

Something is wrong with the (shutter).

(Kuàimén) huài le.

Will you be able to fix it?

Néng xiū ma?

When will it be fixed?

Shénme shíhou néng xiū hăo?

收款台

请用富士相纸。

什么时候取？

能早一点吗？

两天后我就走了。

我想退货。

它坏了。

你们修照相机吗？

快门坏了。

能修吗？

什么时候能修好？

V: *Xíng. Mài gěi nǐ suàn le.*
All right. I might as well sell it to you.

FEC vs. Renminbi

When you are shopping in free markets, be aware of the value of your Foreign Exchange Certificates (FEC). Many luxury goods and imported items can only be bought with FEC, and local Chinese cannot acquire FEC except through foreigners. You can often get a good bargain by offering a vendor FEC instead of local renminbi.

Be wary of black market dealers, however. Tourists these days are often met with cries of "Change money, change money?" Even though the exchange rate (of local renminbi for FEC) might sound good, remember that this activity is illegal. Also, when you leave China, you cannot change that renminbi into any other currency—you'll be stuck with cash you can't spend anywhere else.

What You'll Hear

bú mài	not for sale
Duōdà de?	How large?
huài le	broken
Jǐ hào de?	What size?
jiāo qián	pay
mài wán le	sold out
méi huò	out of stock
Nín yào shénme?	May I help you?
shōukuǎnchù	cashier's booth
yàngpǐn	sample
Zhǐ yǒu zhè yí gè.	It's the only one left.

Signs

bǎihuò shāngdiàn

Department Store

gōngyì měishù shāngdiàn

Arts and Crafts Store

dà jiǎnjià

Reduced Prices

shōu kuǎn tái

Cashier's Booth

yíngyè shíjiān

Business Hours

Entertainment

Zài lái yí gè!
Encore!

While in China, you can enjoy various kinds of evening entertainment. Most cities will have a few cultural performances going on each night, with the major cities offering many. The possibilities range from theater to song and dance, acrobatics, traditional Chinese music, and local opera. Occasionally you might even luck in

Choosing a Show

I'd like to see a (play).	*Wǒ xiǎng kàn (huàjù).*
I'm very interested in (local opera).	*Wǒ duì (dìfāng xì) hěn gǎnxìngqù.*
Is the (performer) famous in China?	*Nèi wèi (yǎnyuán) zài Zhōngguó yǒumíng ma?*
When does the (concert) begin?	*(Yīnyuèhuì) shénme shíhou kāishǐ?*
May I bring a (tape recorder)?	*Wǒ néng dài (lùyīnjī) ma?*
When will the (show) be over?	*(Jiémù) shénme shíhou jiéshù?*
May we leave at (intermission)?	*Wǒmen néng zài (mùjiān xiūxi shí) líkāi ma?*
What (movie) is showing today?	*Jīntiān yǎn shénme (diànyǐng)?*
Is it in English?	*Shì Yīngwén duìbái ma?*
Are there English subtitles?	*Yǒu Yīngwén zìmù ma?*

Buying Tickets

I'd like (two) tickets for [tomorrow].	*Wǒ yào mǎi (liǎng) zhāng [míngtiān] de piào.*
In the (front section), please.	*Qǐng gěi wǒ (qiánpái) de.*

Getting Seated

Excuse me, where are these seats?	*Duìbuqǐ, wǒmen de zuòwèi zài nǎr?*
What are your seat ~~numbe~~rs?	*Nǐmen de zuòwèi hào shì duōshao?*
	~~...shì~~ wǒmen de zuòwèi.

我想看话剧。

我对地方戏很感兴趣。

那位演员在中国有名吗？

音乐会什么时候开始？

我能带录音机吗？

节目什么时候结束？

我们能在幕间休息时离开吗？

今天演什么电影？

是英文对白吗？

有英文字幕吗？

我要买两张明天的票。

请给我前排的。

对不起，我们的座位在哪儿？

你们的座位号是多少？

这是我们的座位。

那儿有人吗？

Musical Instruments

China's musical instruments have a long history. Some of them, such as the *sè* and the *shēng*, date from at least the Warring States Period (475-221 BC). When you go to a concert of traditional Chinese music, you can look for these instruments.

笛子	dízi	8-stop bamboo flute
二胡	èrhú	2-stringed fiddle, with lower register
古琴	gǔqín	7-stringed zither
京胡	jīnghú	2-stringed fiddle, with higher register
琵琶	pípa	4-stringed lute
三弦	sānxián	3-stringed guitar
瑟	sè	25-stringed zither
笙	shēng	Chinese mouth organ
唢呐	suǒnà	Chinese cornet (woodwind)
箫	xiāo	vertical bamboo flute
洋琴	yángqín	dulcimer
月琴	yuèqín	4-stringed round mandolin
筝	zhēng	many-stringed zither

Chinese Operas

There are many local Chinese operas, each with its own colorful style of music, dance, and costume. The six major ones are described below.

Peking Opera: Developed in the mid-nineteenth century when Peking was the capital of the Qing dynasty, this opera's lively repertoire includes many stories about political and military struggles.

continued

ENTERTAINMENT

| There is someone here already. | *Zhèr yǐjīng yǒu rén le.* |
| Where can I get a (program)? | *Nǎr yǒu (jiémùdān)?* |

Asking for Background

Who is (the director)?	*(Dǎoyǎn) shì shéi?*
Who plays (the Emperor)?	*Shéi yǎn (huángdì).*
What is the name of this (song-and-dance troupe)?	*Zhè shì neīge (gēwǔtuán)?*
(Where) was the film shot?	*Zhè bù diànyǐng zài (nǎr) pāi de?*
(When) does the story take place?	*Zhè gùshi fāshēng zài (shénme shíjiān)?*
What (region) is this dance from?	*Zhè shì shénme (dìfang) de wǔdǎo?*
How old are those (acrobats)?	*Zhèxiē (zájì yǎnyuán) duōdà le?*
How long have they (trained)?	*Tāmen (xùnliàn) le duōcháng shíjiān?*
Which (team) is that?	*Nà shì neǐge (duì)?*
What's the score?	*Bǐfēn shì duōshao?*

Showing Appreciation

This (music) is great.	*Zhè (yīnyuè) zhēn bàng!*
Where can I get a (tape) of it?	*Nǎr mài tāde (lùyīndài)?*
The (show) was outstanding.	*Zhège (jiémù) hěn chūsè.*
It's been a really (pleasant) evening.	*Jīnwǎn guò de zhēn (yúkuài).*
I enjoyed it very much.	*Wǒ fēicháng xǐhuan.*

这儿已经有人了。

哪儿有节目单？

导演是谁？

谁演皇帝？

这是哪个歌舞团？

这部电影在哪儿拍的？

这故事发生在什么时间？

这是什么地方的舞蹈？

这些杂技演员多大了？

他们训练了多长时间？

那是哪个队？

比分是多少？

这音乐真棒！

哪儿卖它的录音带？

这个节目很出色。

今晚过得真愉快。

我非常喜欢。

Pingju Opera: Popular in northeastern areas such as Beijing, Tianjin, and Hebei, this is a lively and easy-to-understand folk opera.

Henan Opera: The rustic tunes of this opera are popular in Henan, Shaanxi, Shanxi, Hebei, Shandong, and Anhui Provinces.

Kunshan Opera: With clear singing and gentle gestures, this is one of the oldest traditional operas in China. It originated in the Kunshan area of Jiangsu Province.

Shaoxing Opera: The lyrical tunes of this opera originated from the folk songs of Shengxian County in Zhejiang Province.

Cantonese Opera: This opera has rich musical instrumentation and is popular in Guangdong, Guangxi, Taiwan, Hong Kong, and Macao.

What You'll Hear

guānzhòng	audience
Hǎo!	Bravo!
Hǎo qiú!	Good shot! (sports)
Jiāyóu!	Faster! Go! (sports)
nǚshìmen, xiānshengmen	ladies and gentlemen
Qǐng suí wǒ lái.	Please follow me.
xiūxi (shí) fēnzhōng	(ten)-minute intermission
Yǎnchū dào cǐ jiéshù.	The performance is now over.
Yǎnchū xiànzài kāishǐ.	The performance shall now begin.
Zài lái yí gè!	Encore!

Signs

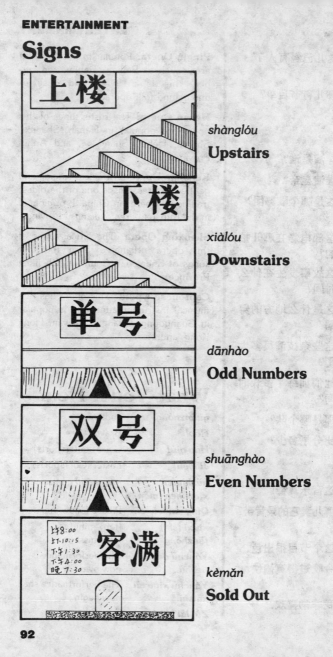

shànglóu
Upstairs

xiàlóu
Downstairs

dānhào
Odd Numbers

shuānghào
Even Numbers

kèmǎn
Sold Out

+ shí **10** Health

> **Wǒ tóuténg.**
> I've got a headache.

Hopefully you will never have to use this chapter, but...if you ever do feel under the weather, the best thing to do is to take care of the illness quickly. Large hotels usually have a clinic or doctor's office for just that purpose. Once there, you will first be asked your name, age, nationality, and cities recently visited. Then it will be time to describe your complaints. The doctor may only know a few medical terms in English, so bear in mind the phrases here.

HEALTH

Getting Help

I need to (see a dentist).	*Wǒ yào (kàn yá).*
Where is the (clinic)?	*(Yīwùsuǒ) zài nǎr?*
Please take me to the (hospital).	*Qǐng dài wǒ qù (yīyuàn).*
When does the (clinic) open?	*(Yīwùsuǒ) shénme shíhou kāimén?*
Do they understand English?	*Tāmen dǒng Yīngwén ma?*

Complaints

It hurts when I (talk).	*Yì (shuōhuà) jiù téng.*
It hurts here.	*Zhèr téng.*
I don't feel well.	*Wǒ juéde bù shūfu.*
I feel (faint).	*Wǒ (tóuyūn)*
I have a cold.	*Wǒ gǎnmào le.*
I'm allergic to (pencillin).	*Wǒ duì (qīngméisù) guòmǐn.*
I have (diabetes).	*Wǒ yǒu (tángniàobìng).*
I have (a cardiac condition).	*Wǒ yǒu (xīnzàngbìng).*
I'm pregnant.	*Wǒ huáiyùn le.*

Requests

Please take my (temperature).	*Qǐng tì wǒ liáng yíxià (tǐwēn).*
Please give me some (medicine).	*Qǐng gěi wǒ diǎn (yào).*
I need some (aspirin).	*Wǒ yào diǎn (āsīpǐlín).*

Questions

Is it (a contagious disease)?	*Shì (chuánrǎnbìng) ma?*

我要看牙。

医务所在哪儿?

请带我去医院。

医务所什么时候开门?

他们懂英文吗?

一说话就疼。

这儿疼。

我觉得不舒服。

我头晕。

我感冒了。

我对青霉素过敏。

我有糖尿病。

我有心脏病。

我怀孕了。

请替我量一下体温。

请给我点药。

我要点阿斯匹林。

是传染病吗?

Where Does It Hurt?

When telling the doctor where you have pain, the best method is to point to the afflicted area. You can also try using the Chinese words below.

ankle: *jiǎowàn*	脚腕
back: *bèibù*	背部
bone: *gútou*	骨头
ear: *ěrduo*	耳朵
eye: *yǎnjīng*	眼睛
hand: *shǒu*	手
head: *tóu*	头
heart: *xīnzàng*	心脏
hip: *kuà*	胯
joint: *guānjié*	关节
knee: *xīgài*	膝盖
leg: *tuǐ*	腿
muscle: *jīròu*	肌肉
neck: *bózi*	脖子
shoulder: *jiānbǎng*	肩膀
stomach: *wèi*	胃
throat: *hóulóng*	喉咙
tooth: *yáchǐ*	牙齿

Doctor, I Have...

Many of the common ailments of China travelers are due to the change of environment plus the fatigue of being on the road. The doctor will prescribe either traditional herbal medicines (quite effective) or Western pharmaceuticals. Here's how to describe your symptoms:

I have...
    Wǒ...   我···

a cold
    gǎnmào le   感冒了

continued

HEALTH

Can I (travel) tomorrow?	*Míngtiān wǒ néng (qù lǚxíng) ma?*
How long will this (illness) last?	*Zhèige (bìng) shénme shíhou néng hǎo?*
How should this medicine be taken?	*Zhèige yào zěnme chī fǎ?*
Should I take all this medicine?	*Zhèxiē yào dōu chī le ma?*
Do I need to come back for another session?	*Wǒ hái yào zài lái kàn ma?*

Taking Leave

I feel much better now.	*Wǒ gǎnjué hǎo duō le.*
Thank you, doctor.	*Xièxie nín, dàifu.*

明天我能去旅行吗？

这个病什么时候能好？

这个药怎么吃法？

这些药都吃了吗？

我还要再来看吗？

我感觉好多了。

谢谢您，大夫。

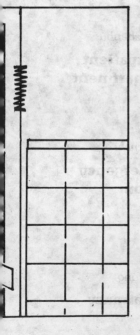

constipation	*yǒu diǎn biànmì*	有点便秘
a cough	*yǒu diǎn késou*	有点咳嗽
diarrhea	*lā dùzi*	拉肚子
a fever	*fāshāo*	发烧
a headache	*tóuténg*	头疼
indigestion	*xiāohuà bù liáng*	消化不良
an infection	*fāyán le*	发炎了
insomnia	*shīmián*	失眠
nasal congestion	*bízi bù tōngqì*	鼻子不通气
a sore throat	*hóulóng tòng*	喉咙疼
a sprained ankle	*jiǎowàn niǔ le*	脚腕扭了

What You'll Hear

dǎzhēn	injection
jiā zài yèxià	put under your arm
liáng tǐwēn	take a temperature
měicì chī...	each time take...
Nǎli bù shūfu?	Where is the discomfort?
pào zài rèshuǐ lǐ	steep in hot water
tǎng xià	lie down
xiūxi	rest
yàofāng	prescription
yì tiān chī (sān) cì	take it (three) times a day

Signs

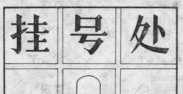

rénmín yīyuàn
People's Hospital

guàhào chù
Registration Office

ménzhěnbù
Outpatient Department

jízhěnshì
Emergency Room

yàofáng
Pharmacy

English-Chinese Dictionary

This is a simplified dictionary for the China traveler. The Chinese expressions here are colloquial equivalents, not academic translations, of the English entries. Where an entry has several meanings, a clarification of the intended meaning appears in parentheses. Abbreviations used are: noun (n), verb (v), and adjective (adj). Be aware that some Chinese expressions cannot be used syntactically like the corresponding English. However, they can be used effectively as replacements within the sentence patterns of the text.

a, an	yī, yígè	一，一个
a few	jǐgè	几个
a little	yìdiǎn	一点
a while	yíhuǐr	一会儿
about (approximately)	dàyuē	大约
about (concerning)	guānyú	关于
above	zài...zhī shàng	在······之上
accept	jiēshòu	接受
accident	shìgù, yìwài	事故，意外
accompaniment (music)	bànzòu	伴奏
accompany	péi	陪
accordion	shǒufēngqín	手风琴
accurate	zhèngquè, zhǔnquè	正确，准确
achievement	chéngjì, chéngguǒ	成绩，成果
acre	yīngmǔ	英亩
acrid	sè	涩
acrobat	zájì yǎnyuán	杂技演员
acrobatics	zájì	杂技
acrylic (fiber)	bǐnglún	丙纶
acting (performance)	biǎoyǎn	表演
action	xíngdòng, dòngzuò	行动，动作
activity	huódòng	活动
actor (actress)	yǎnyuán	演员
acupressure	diǎnxuè fǎ	点穴法
acupuncture	zhēnjiǔ	针灸

DICTIONARY

acupuncture anesthesia	*zhēncì mázuì*	针刺麻醉
acute	*jíxìng*	急性
adaptor (outlet board)	*jiēxiànbǎn*	接线板
adaptor (outlet cube)	*sāntōng*	三通
adaptor plug	*zhuǎnjiē chātóu*	转接插头
add	*jiā*	加
address (n)	*dìzhǐ*	地址
addressee	*shōujiàn rén, duìfāng*	收件人，对方
adhesive plaster	*xiàngpí gāo*	橡皮膏
adjust	*tiáo*	调
adjustment	*tiáozhěng*	调整
administrator	*guǎnlǐ zhě*	管理者
adore	*rè'ài*	热爱
adult	*chéngrén, dàrén*	成人，大人
advanced	*xiānjìn*	先进
advertisement manager	*guǎnggào jīnglǐ*	广告经理
aerobics	*jiànměi cāo*	健美操
affair (matter)	*shìqing*	事情
afraid	*pà*	怕
Africa	*Fēizhōu*	非洲
after meals	*fànhòu*	饭后
afternoon	*xiàwǔ*	下午
again	*zài*	再
agate	*mǎnǎo*	玛瑙
age (of a person)	*niánlíng*	年龄
agriculture	*nóngyè*	农业
AIDS	*àizī bìng*	爱滋病
air	*kōngqì*	空气
air conditioner	*kōngtiáojī*	空调机
air conditioning	*kōngtiáo*	空调
air force	*kōngjūn*	空军
air pump	*qìbèng, qìtǒng*	气泵，气筒
air sick	*yūnjī*	晕机
air valve	*qìfá, qìmén*	气阀，气门
airline	*hángkōng gōngsī*	航空公司
airmail	*hángkōng*	航空
airplane	*fēijī*	飞机
airport	*fēijīchǎng*	飞机场
airport departure tax	*jīchǎng fèi*	机场费

aisle	guòdào	过道
alarm clock	nàozhōng	闹钟
alcohol (fluid)	jiǔjīng	酒精
alcohol (liquor)	jiǔ	酒
alike	yíyàng, xiàng	一样，象
all	quánbù, dōu	全部，都
allergic	guòmǐn	过敏
allergy	guòmǐn zhèng	过敏症
alley	hútong	胡同
allspice	làméi	腊梅
almond	xìngrén	杏仁
almond-flour tea	xìngrénchá	杏仁茶
almond gelatin	xìngrén dòufu	杏仁豆腐
alone	dāndú	单独
already	yǐjīng	已经
also	yě	也
altitude	hǎibá	海拔
altogether	yígòng	一共
always	zǒngshì, lǎoshì	总是，老是
ambulance	jiùhùchē	救护车
analyze	fēnxī	分析
ancient	gǔdài	古代
and	hé, gēn	和，跟
anemia	pínxuě zhèng	贫血症
anesthesia	mázuì	麻醉
anesthetist	mázuì shī	麻醉师
angina pectoris	xīn jiǎotòng	心绞痛
angry	shēngqì	生气
animal	dòngwù	动物
ankle	jiǎowàn	脚腕
anniversary	zhōunián	周年
another	lìng yí gè, biéde	另一个，别的
answer (phone)	jiē	接…
answer (reply)	huídá	回答
ant	mǎyǐ	蚂蚁
antenna (for TV, radio)	tiānxiàn	天线
anthropology	rénlèixué	人类学
antibiotic	kàngshēngsù	抗生素
antipyretic	tuìshāo	退烧
antique	gǔdǒng	古董
antiseptic cream	xiāodú gāo	消毒膏

DICTIONARY

anxious	zhāojí	着急
any	rènhé	任何
apartment	dānyuán fáng, gōngyù	单元房，公寓
appetite	wèikǒu	胃口
applause	gǔzhǎng	鼓掌
apple	píngguǒ	苹果
apply for	shēnqǐng	申请
appreciate	xīnshǎng	欣赏
apprentice	xuétú	学徒
appropriate	héshì	合适
apricot	xìng	杏
April	sìyuè	四月
archaeology	kǎogǔ	考古
architecture	jiànzhù	建筑
area (measure)	miànjī	面积
area (realm)	lǐngyù, fànwéi	领域，范围
area (region)	dìqū	地区
argali sheep	tānyáng	滩羊
arm	gēbo, shǒubì	胳膊，手臂
armband	bìzhāng	臂章
armpit	yè	腋
army	bùduì, jūnduì	部队，军队
around (approximately)	zuǒyòu	左右
arrange	ānpái	安排
arrangement	ānpái	安排
arrive	dàodá	到达
art	yìshù	艺术
art director	yìshù zhǐdǎo	艺术指导
art exhibition	měishù zhǎnlǎn	美术展览
art gallery	huàláng	画廊
art museum	měishùguǎn	美术馆
art work	yìshùpǐn	艺术品
arthritis	guānjiéyán	关节炎
article (object)	wùpǐn	物品
arts and crafts	gōngyì měishù	工艺美术
arts and crafts store	gōngyì měishù shāngdiàn	工艺美术商店
ashtray	yānhuīgāng	烟灰缸
Asia	Yàzhōu	亚洲
ask	wèn	问
asparagus lettuce	wōsǔn	莴笋
aspen tree	báiyángshù	白杨树

aspirin	āsīpǐlín	阿斯匹林
assistant (n)	zhùshǒu, zhùlǐ	助手，助理
assistant manager (hotel)	dàtáng jīnglǐ	大堂经理
assorted	jīngxuǎn	精选
assorted cold dishes	lěng pīnpán	冷拼盘
asthma	qìchuǎn	气喘
at	zài	在
athlete	yùndòngyuán	运动员
Atlantic Ocean	Dàxīyáng	大西洋
atomic	yuánzǐ	原子
attend class	shàngkè	上课
attend school	shàngxué	上学
attention	zhùyì	注意
audience	guānzhòng	观众
auditorium	lǐtáng	礼堂
August	bāyuè	八月
aunt (see Appendix H)	āyí	阿姨
Australia	Àodàlìyà	澳大利亚
Australian dollar	àoyuán	澳元
author	zuòzhě	作者
automatic	zìdòng	自动
autumn	qiūtiān	秋天
avenue	dàjiē	大街
awhile	yìhuǐr	一会儿
azalea	dùjuānhuā	杜鹃花
back (direction)	hòu	后
back (n)	bèi	背
back door	hòumén	后门
back section (seating)	hòupái	后排
backpack	shuāngjiān kuàbāo	双肩挎包
backstage	hòutái	后台
backyard	hòuyuàn	后院
bad	huài	坏
badminton	yǔmáoqiú	羽毛球
bag	dài, dàizi	袋，袋子
baggage	xíngli	行李
baggage cart	xíngli chē	行李车
baggage claim area	xíngli tīng	行李厅
baggage claim office	xíngli bàngōngshì	行李办公室
baggage strap	xíngli dài	行李带

DICTIONARY

baggage tag	*xíngli pái*	行李牌
balcony (seating)	*lóushàng zuòwei*	楼上座位
balcony (terrace)	*yángtái*	阳台
Bali	*Bālì*	巴厘
ball	*qiú*	球
ball game	*qiúsài*	球赛
ballet	*bāléiwǔ*	芭蕾舞
ballpoint pen	*yuánzhūbǐ*	圆珠笔
ballroom	*wǔtīng*	舞厅
bamboo	*zhúzi*	竹子
bamboo shoot	*zhúsǔn*	竹笋
bambooware	*zhúbiān*	竹编
banana	*xiāngjiāo*	香蕉
band (music group)	*yuèduì*	乐队
band (radio)	*bōduàn*	播段
Band-Aid	*zhǐxuè jiāobù*	止血胶布
bandage (n)	*bēngdài*	绷带
Bangkok	*Màngǔ*	曼谷
bank (financial)	*yínháng*	银行
banquet	*yànhuì*	宴会
banquet manager	*yànhuìtīng jīnglǐ*	宴会厅经理
banyan tree	*róngshù*	榕树
bar (for drinks)	*jiǔbā*	酒吧
barber shop	*lǐfà diàn*	理发店
bargain prices	*yìjià*	议价
barley	*dàmài, qīngkē*	大麦,青稞
baseball	*bàngqiú*	棒球
basin (land)	*péndì*	盆地
basketball	*lánqiú*	兰球
bat	*biānfú*	蝙蝠
bath towel	*yùjīn*	浴巾
bathhouse	*zǎotáng*	澡堂
bathroom (for baths)	*yùshì*	浴室
bathroom (toilet)	*cèsuǒ*	厕所
bathtub	*yùchí*	浴池
batik	*làrǎn*	蜡染
battery	*diànchí*	电池
bayberry, red	*yángméi*	杨梅
be	*shì*	是
bean	*dòuzi*	豆子
bean paste	*dòushā*	豆沙
bean sauce, hot	*dòubàn jiàng*	豆瓣酱

bean sprout	dòuyá	豆芽
beancurd	dòufu	豆腐
bear (n)	xióng, gǒuxióng	熊, 狗熊
beautiful	měilì, piàoliang	美丽, 漂亮
beauty salon	fàláng	发廊
beaver	hǎilí	海狸
because	yīnwéi	因为
bed	chuáng	床
bedroom	wòshì	卧室
bedtime	shuìjiào shíjiān	睡觉时间
beef	niúròu	牛肉
beefsteak	niúpái	牛排
beer	píjiǔ	啤酒
beet	tiáncài	甜菜
before	yǐqián	以前
before meals	fànqián	饭前
before sleep	shuìqián	睡前
beggar	qǐgài	乞丐
begin	kāishǐ	开始
begonia	qiūhǎitáng	秋海棠
Beijing Opera	jīngjù	京剧
Belgium	Bǐlìshí	比利时
believe (faith)	xiāngxìn	相信
believe (opinion)	rènwéi	认为
bell (ancient)	gǔzhōng	古钟
bell captain	xíngli lǐngbān	行李领班
bell tower	zhōnglóu	钟楼
belong to	shǔyú	属于
below	zài...xiàmiàn	在……下面
Berlin	Bólín	柏林
berth	chuángwèi	床位
best	zuìhǎo	最好
better	gènghǎo	更好
bicycle	zìxíngchē	自行车
big	dà	大
bill (money notes)	piàozi	票子
bill (payment due)	zhàngdān	帐单
billiards	táiqiú	台球
billion	shíyì	十亿
biology	shēngwùxué	生物学
bird	niǎo	鸟
birthday	shēngrì	生日

DICTIONARY

biscuit	bǐnggān	饼干
bite (v)	yǎo	咬
bitter	kǔ	苦
bitter gourd	kǔguā	苦瓜
black	hēi	黑
black mushroom	xiānggū, dōnggū	香菇, 冬菇
black tea	hóngchá	红茶
black-and-white	hēibái	黑白
blackboard	hēibǎn	黑板
bland	dàn	淡
blank tape	kòngbái dài	空白带
blanket (n)	tǎnzi	毯子
bleed	liúxuè	流血
blister	pào	疱
blocked (stopped up)	dǔsè	堵塞
blonde	jīnfà	金发
blood	xuěyè	血液
blood pressure	xuěyā	血压
blood type	xuèxíng	血型
blouse	nǔ chènshān	女衬衫
blow dry	chuīgān	吹干
blow dryer	chuīfēngjī	吹风机
blue	lán	蓝
blunt (dull)	dùn	钝
board game	qísài	棋赛
boarding pass	dēngjī pái	登机牌
boat	chuán, zhōu	船, 舟
boat ride	chèngchuán	乘船
body (human)	shēntǐ	身体
boil (v)	shāokāi, zhǔ	烧开, 煮
boiled dumplings	shuǐjiǎo	水饺
boiled egg	zhǔ jīdàn	煮鸡蛋
boiled water	kāishuǐ	开水
bok choy	báicài	白菜
bon voyage	yīlù shùnfēng	一路顺风
bone	gǔtou	骨头
Bonn	Bō'ēn	波恩
bonsai	pénjǐng	盆景
bonus	jiǎngjīn	奖金
book (n)	shū	书
booking office	dìngpiào chù	订票处
bookkeeper	kuàijì	会计

bookstore	shūdiàn	书店
boring	kūzào	枯燥
borrow	jiè	借
Boston	Bōshìdùn	波士顿
bottle (n)	píngzi	瓶子
bottle opener	pínggài qǐzi	瓶盖起子
bourgeois	zīchǎn jiējí	资产阶级
bowel movement	dàbiàn	大便
bowels	chángzi	肠子
bowl (n)	wǎn	碗
bowling	bǎolíngqiú	保龄球
bowling alley	bǎolíng qiúchǎng	保龄球场
box (carton)	hézi	盒子
box office	shòupiàochù	售票处
boxing	quánjī	拳击
boy	nánhái	男孩
boyfriend	nán péngyǒu	男朋友
bracelet	shǒuzhuó	手镯
brakes	zhá, sāchē	闸，刹车
brandy	báilándì	白兰地
brass instrument	tóngguǎn yuèqì	铜管乐器
Bravo!	Hǎo!	好！
bread	miànbāo	面包
breakdancing	pīlì wǔ	霹雳舞
breakfast	zǎofàn	早饭
breathe	hūxī	呼吸
brick	zhuāntou	砖头
brick tea	zhuānchá	砖茶
bridge (n)	qiáo	桥
bright	liàng, xiānyàn	亮，鲜艳
brightness	liàngdù	亮度
bring	dài, ná	带，拿
Britain	Yīngguó	英国
broad bean	cándòu	蚕豆
broadcasting station	guǎngbō diàntái	广播电台
brocade	zhījǐn	织锦
broccoli, Chinese	gàilán	芥蓝
broken (out of order)	huài le	坏了
broken (severed)	duàn le	断了
bronchitis	zhī qìguǎn yán	支气管炎
bronze chariot	tóng zhànchē	铜战车
broom	tiáozhou	笤帚

DICTIONARY

broth	qīngtāng	清汤
brother (older)	gēge	哥哥
brother (younger)	dìdi	弟弟
brown	zōngsè	棕色
brown paper	niúpí zhǐ	牛皮纸
brown sauce (braised in)	hóngshāo	红烧
brush	shuāzi	刷子
Brussels	Bùlǔsài'ěr	布鲁塞尔
bubble gum	pàopaotáng	泡泡糖
buddha	fó	佛
buddhism	fójiào	佛教
building (n)	lóufáng, jiànzhù	楼房,建筑
bull	gōngniú	公牛
Bund (Shanghai)	Wàitān	外滩
bureau (organization)	jú	局
bureau director	júzhǎng	局长
burial grounds	mùdì	墓地
Burma	Miǎndiàn	缅甸
burn (n)	shāoshāng	烧伤
bus (n)	qìchē	汽车
bus driver	sījī	司机
bus map	qìchē xiànlù tú	汽车线路图
bus station	qìchē zǒngzhàn	汽车总站
bus stop	qìchē zhàn	汽车站
bushel	pǔshì'ěr	蒲式耳
business	shēngyì	生意
business management	qǐyè guǎnlǐ	企业管理
business person	shāngrén	商人
busy	máng	忙
busy line (phone)	zhànxiàn	占线
but	dànshì	但是
butcher shop	ròudiàn	肉店
butter	huángyóu	黄油
buttocks	pìgu	屁股
button (for clothing)	kòuzi	扣子
button (pushbutton)	ànniǔ	按纽
buy	mǎi	买
CAAC	Zhōngguó mínháng	中国民航
cabbage	yáng báicài	洋白菜

cabbage heart	càixīn	菜心
cabbage, Chinese	dà báicài	大白菜
cabin (ship)	cāng, chuáncāng	舱，船舱
cable address	diànbào guàhào	电报挂号
cable TV	bìlù diànshì	闭路电视
cadre	gànbù	干部
cadre's jacket	zhōngshān zhuāng	中山装
cafe	kāfēiguǎn	咖啡馆
cake	dàngāo	蛋糕
calendar	rìlì	日历
California	Jiāzhōu	加州
call (to beckon)	jiào	叫
call (to telephone)	gěi...dǎdiànhuà	给……打电话
calligrapher	shūfǎjiā	书法家
calligraphy	shūfǎ	书法
calligraphy brush	máobǐ	毛笔
camel	luòtuo	骆驼
camelia	cháhuā	茶花
camera	zhàoxiàngjī	照像机
camphor tree	zhāngshù	樟树
can (know how to)	huì	会
can (possible to)	néng	能
can (tin, jar)	guàntou	罐头
can opener	guàntou qǐzi	罐头起子
Canada	Jiānádà	加拿大
canal	yùnhé	运河
cancel	qǔxiāo	取消
cancer	áizhèng	癌症
candied haws	bīngtáng húlu	冰糖葫芦
candy	táng, tángguǒ	糖，糖果
canoe	dúmùzhōu	独木舟
Canon	Jiā néng	佳能
Cantonese Opera	yuèjù	粤剧
capital (city)	shǒudū	首都
capital (money)	zījīn, zīběn	资金，资本
capitalist (n)	zīběnjiā	资本家
capon	yānjī	阉鸡
capsule	jiāonáng	胶囊
caption	zìmù	字幕
car	qìchē, xiǎojiàochē	汽车，小轿车
car sick	yūnchē	晕车
cardiac failure	xīnlì shuāijié	心力衰竭

DICTIONARY

cardiology	xīnzàng bìngxué	心脏病学
cards (playing)	púkè pái	扑克牌
career	shìyè	事业
careful	xiǎoxīn	小心
careless	mǎdàhā	马大哈
carpenter	mùjiàng	木匠
carpet	dìtǎn	地毯
carrot	húluóbo	胡萝卜
carry	xiédài	携带
carry-on luggage	shǒutí xínglǐ	手提行李
cart (n)	tuīchē	推车
cartoon (film)	dònghuà piān	动画片
cartoon (print)	mànhuà	漫画
carving (n)	diāokè	雕刻
cash (n)	xiànjīn	现金
cash (v)	duìhuàn	兑换
cash advance	xiànjīn yùfù	现金预付
cashew nut	yāoguǒ	腰果
cashier	chū nà yuán	出纳员
cashier's booth	shōukuǎnchù	收款处
cashmere	kāishìmǐ	开士米
casserole	shāguō	沙锅
cassette (sound tape)	cídài	磁带
cassia	guìhuā	桂花
cassia wine	guìhuā jiǔ	桂花酒
casual	suíbiàn	随便
cat	māo	猫
catch (v)	zhuāzhù	抓住
cathartic	xièyào	泻药
cattle	shēngkou	牲口
cauliflower	càihuā	菜花
cave	shāndòng	山洞
CCTV English Service	diànshì yīngyǔ jiému	电视英语节目
ceiling	tiānhuābǎn	天花板
celery	qíncài	芹菜
cellophane tape	tòumíng jiāodài	透明胶带
cement (concrete)	shuǐní	水泥
center (middle)	zhōngjiān	中间
centigrade	shèshì	摄氏
centimeter	límǐ	厘米
Central America	Zhōngměizhōu	中美洲

century	shìjì	世纪
ceramics	táocí	陶瓷
certain	yídìng	一定
certificate	zhèngmíng	证明
chain	liàntiáo, liànzi	链条，链子
chair (n)	yǐzi	椅子
chairman	zhǔxí	主席
Chairman Mao	Máo zhǔxí	毛主席
chamber music	shìnèi yuè	室内乐
champagne	xiāngbīnjiǔ	香槟酒
champion	guànjūn	冠军
chance (opportunity)	jīhuì	机会
change (coins, small bills)	língqián	零钱
change (to replace, exchange)	huàn	换
change (transfer)	diào	调
change (transformation)	biànhuà	变化
channel (TV)	píndào	频道
character (role)	juésè	角色
characteristic	tèdiǎn	特点
charcoal drawing	tànhuà	炭画
charge d'affaires	lǐngshì	领事
charming	mírén	迷人
cheap	piányi	便宜
cheapest	zuìpiányi	最便宜
check, bank	zhīpiào	支票
check in (for flight)	bàn chéngjī shǒuxù	办乘机手续
check in (register)	dēngjì	登记
check out (from a hotel)	tuìfáng	退房
checkers, Chinese	tiàoqí	跳棋
Cheers!	Gānbēi!	干杯！
cheese	nǎilào	奶酪
chef	chúshī	厨师
chemical (adj)	huàxué	化学
chemist's (drugstore)	yàodiàn	药店
chemistry	huàxué	化学
chemotherapy	huàliáo	化疗
cheongsam (gown)	qípáo	旗袍
cherry	yīngtáo	樱桃

chess	guójì xiàngqí	国际象棋
chess, Chinese	xiàngqí	象棋
chest pain	xiōngkǒu tòng	胸口疼
chestnut	lìzi	栗子
chewing gum	kǒuxiāngtáng	口香糖
Chicago	Zhījiāgē	芝加哥
chicken	jī	鸡
child	xiǎohái	小孩
children's clothing	tóngzhuāng	童装
children's palace	shàonián gōng	少年宫
chilli pepper (dried)	gān làjiāo	干辣椒
China	Zhōngguó	中国
China Central Television (CCTV)	Zhōngyāng diànshì tái	中央电视台
Chinese (language)	Hànyǔ	汉语
Chinese character	Hànzì	汉字
Chinese meal	zhōngcān	中餐
Chinese menu	zhōngcān càipǔ	中餐菜谱
Chinese New Year	chūnjié	春节
chives, Chinese	jiǔcài	韭菜
chocolate	qiǎokèlì	巧克力
choice	xuǎnzé	选择
cholera	huòluàn	霍乱
choose	xuǎn, tiāo	选，挑
chop (seal)	yìnzhāng shí, túzhāng	印章石，图章
chopsticks	kuàizi	筷子
chorus	héchàng	合唱
Christmas	Shèngdànjié	圣诞节
chronic	mànxìng	慢性
chrysanthemum	júhuā	菊花
chrysolite (jade)	fěicuì	翡翠
church	jiàotáng	教堂
cigarette	xiāngyān	香烟
cinema	diànyǐng yuàn	电影院
circle (n)	quān	圈
circus	mǎxì	马戏
citizen	gōngmín	公民
city	chéngshì	城市
city gate	chéngmén	城门
city map	chéngshì jiāotōng tú	城市交通图
city tour	yóulǎn shìróng	游览市容
civil	mínyòng	民用

clams	géli	蛤蜊
clap (applaud)	gǔzhǎng	鼓掌
class (social)	jiējí	阶级
class (students)	bān	班
classic	gǔdiǎn	古典
classroom	jiàoshì, kètáng	教室，课堂
clay	niántǔ	粘土
clay figure	nírén	泥人
clean (adj)	gānjìng	干净
clean (v)	dǎsǎo	打扫
cleaning solution	xiāodú yè	消毒液
clear (distinct)	qīngchǔ	清楚
climb	pá	爬
clinic	wèishēngsuǒ	卫生所
clock	zhōng	钟
cloisonne	jīngtàilán	景泰蓝
cloisonne vase	jīngtàilán huāpíng	景泰蓝花瓶
close (to shut)	guān	关
closed (business)	guānmén	关门
closed (not public)	bù kāifàng	不开放
closet	yīguì	衣柜
cloth	bù, liàozi	布，料子
clothespin	yīfujiā	衣服夹
clothing	yīfu	衣服
clothing store	fùzhuāng diàn	服装店
cloud	yún	云
cloudyweather	yīn duōyún	阴，多云
club (recreation)	jùlèbù	俱乐部
coach (sports)	jiàoliàn	教练
coal	méi	煤
coat	shàngyī, dàyī	上衣，大衣
coat hanger	yījià	衣架
Coca-Cola	Kěkǒu Kělè	可口可乐
cocaine	kěkǎyīn	可卡因
cock's comb (flower)	jīguānhuā	鸡冠花
cockroach	zhāngláng	蟑螂
cocoa	kōukou	可可
coconut	yēzi	椰子
cocoon	cánjiǎn	蚕茧
coffee	kāfēi	咖啡
coffee shop	kāfēi diàn	咖啡店
cola	kělè	可乐

DICTIONARY

cold (adj)	lěng	冷
cold (illness)	gǎnmào, zhāoliáng	感冒，着凉
cold drink	lěngyǐn	冷饮
cold drinking water	liángbáikāi	凉白开
cold milk	lěng niúnǎi	冷牛奶
cold platter	lěngpán	冷盘
cold water (from tap)	lěngshuǐ	冷水
cold-water wash	lěngshuǐ xǐ	冷水洗
cold wave (perm)	lěngtàng	冷烫
collect (gather)	shōují	收集
collect (phone call)	duìfāng fùkuǎn	对方付款
college	xuéyuàn, dàxué	学院，大学
color (n)	yánsè	颜色
color TV	cǎidiàn	彩电
colored	cǎisè	彩色
column (pillar)	zhùzi	柱子
coma	hūnmí	昏迷
comb (n)	shūzi	梳子
come	lái	来
comedy	xǐjù	喜剧
comfortable	shūfu	舒服
commemorative stamp	jìniàn yóupiào	纪念邮票
common	pǔtōng	普通
commune	gōngshè	公社
communist party	gòngchǎndǎng	共产党
compact disc	jīguāng chàngpiàn	激光唱片
company (business)	gōngsī	公司
company account	gōngsī zhànghù	公司帐户
complain	bàoyuàn	抱怨
completely	wánquán	完全
composer (music)	zuòqǔjiā	作曲家
composition (music)	zuòpǐn	作品
composition (painting)	gòutú	构图
comprehensive	zōnghé	综合
computer	jìsuànjī, diànnǎo	计算机，电脑
computer programmer	diànnǎo chéngxùyuán	电脑程序员
comrade	tóngzhì	同志
concerning	guānyú	关于
concert	yīnyuèhuì	音乐会

concert hall	yīnyuè tīng	音乐厅
concierge (hotel)	jiēdàiyuán	接待员
concubine	fēizi, qiè	妃子，妾
condition	tiáojiàn, qíngkuàng	条件，情况
conditioner (for hair)	hùfàsù	护发素
conductor (bus)	shòupiàoyuán	售票员
conductor (music)	zhǐhuī	指挥
conductor (train)	chèngwùyuán	乘务员
conference room	huìyìshì	会议室
confirm	quèdìng	确定
connect	jiē	接
connecting flight	xiánjiē hángbān	衔接航班
connection (relation)	guānxi	关系
conscience	liángxīn	良心
consider	kǎolǜ	考虑
consomme	qīngtāng	清汤
constipation	biànbì	便秘
Constitution	xiànfǎ	宪法
construction	jiànshè	建设
contact lens	yǐnxíng yǎnjìng	隐形眼镜
contact prints (photo)	xiǎoyàng	小样
contagious	jiēchù chuánrǎn	接触传染
container	róngqì	容器
contemporary (adj)	dāngdài	当代
continent	dàlù	大陆
contraceptives	bìyùn yòngpǐn	避孕用品
contrast (n)	duìbǐ	对比
convenient	fāngbiàn	方便
convulsion	jīngluán	痉挛
cook (n)	chúshī, dà shīfù	厨师，大师傅
cook (prepare meals)	zuòfàn	做饭
cookie	bǐnggān	饼干
cooking	pēngtiáo	烹调
cool (adj)	liáng, liángkuài	凉，凉快
copy (n)	fùběn	副本
corduroy	dēngxīn róng	灯芯绒
coriander	xiāngcài	香菜
cork carving	ruǎnmù diāo	软木雕
corkscrew	píngsāi qǐzi	瓶塞起子
corn	yùmǐ	玉米
cornet, Chinese	suǒnà	锁呐
corporation	gōngsī	公司

DICTIONARY

correct (yes)	duì	对
costume	xìzhuāng	戏装
cot	zhédié chuáng	折叠床
cottage (thatched)	cǎofáng	草房
cotton	mián	棉
cotton-padded jacket	miányī	棉衣
cotton-padded shoes	miánxié	棉鞋
cough	késòu	咳嗽
cough drops	hánpiàn	含片
cough syrup	zhǐké tángjiāng	止咳糖浆
country (nation)	guójiā	国家
country (rural)	xiāngcūn	乡村
country music	xiāngcūn yīnyuè	乡村音乐
countryside	nóngcūn	农村
county	xiàn	县
courtyard	yuànzi	院子
cover (n)	gàizi	盖子
cow	nǎiniú	奶牛
crab	pángxiè	螃蟹
crabapple, Chinese	hǎitáng	海棠
craft	gōngyì	工艺
craftsman	gōngjiàng	工匠
cramp	chōujīn	抽筋
crane	hè	鹤
crayons	làbǐ	蜡笔
cream (dairy)	nǎiyóu	奶油
creator	chuàngzào zhě	创造者
credit card	xìnyòngkǎ	信用卡
crepe (pancake)	jiānbǐng	煎饼
crispy	cuì	脆
crispy duck	xiāngsū yā	香酥鸭
critical condition	qíngkuàng wēijí	情况危急
crop (n)	nóngzuòwù	农作物
cross (pass)	guò	过
cross talk (comedy routine)	xiàngsheng	相声
crosswalk	rénxíng héngdào	人行横道
cruise (v)	yóu	游
cruise boat	yóutǐng	游艇
cry (sob)	kū	哭
cub	yòuzǎi	幼仔
cucumber	huángguā	黄瓜

cultural exchange	wénhuà jiāoliú	文化交流
cultural relic	wénhuà gǔjì	文化古迹
Cultural Revolution	wéngé	文革
culture (arts, customs)	wénhuà	文化
cup	bēi, bēizi	杯,杯子
curler (for hair)	fàjuǎn	发卷
curling iron	měifà qì	美发器
curly	juǎnqū shì	卷曲式
curry	gāli	咖喱
curtain (theater)	mù	幕
curtain (window)	chuānglián	窗帘
cushion	diànzi	垫子
custom (tradition)	fēngsú	风俗
custom-made	dìngzuò de	订做的
customer	gùkè	顾客
Customs	hǎiguān	海关
customs declaration	hǎiguān shēnbào dān	海关申报单
customs duty	guānshuì	关税
cut (v)	jiǎn, qiē	剪,切
cuttlefish	mòdǒuyú, wūzéi	墨斗鱼,乌贼
cycling	qí zìxíngchē	骑自行车
cymbals	chǎ	钗
cypress tree	bǎishù	柏树
daily (newspaper)	rìbào	日报
Dalai Lama	Dálài Lǎma	达赖喇嘛
dam	dībà	堤坝
damaged	nònghuài le	弄坏了
damp	shī	湿
dance (n)	wǔdǎo	舞蹈
dance (v)	tiàowǔ	跳舞
dance drama	wǔjù	舞剧
dance hall	wǔtīng	舞厅
dance party	wǔhuì	舞会
dance troupe	wǔdǎo tuán	舞蹈团
dancer	wǔdǎo yǎnyuán	舞蹈演员
danger	wēixiǎn	危险
dark	hēi	黑
darkroom	ànshì	暗室
date (appointment)	yuēhuì	约会
date (fruit)	zǎo	枣

DICTIONARY

dating (courtship)	tán liàn'ài	谈恋爱
daughter	nǚér	女儿
day	rì, tiān	日，天
day after tomorrow	hòutiān	后天
day-lily bud	jīnzhēn	金针
daytime	báitiān	白天
deaf	lóng	聋
December	shí'èryuè	十二月
decide	juédìng	决定
declare (at Customs)	shēnbào	申报
decongestant	bítōng	鼻通
decoration	zhuāngshì	装饰
deep	shēn	深
deep-fried	zhá	炸
deer	lù	鹿
degree (temperature)	dù	度
delicatessen	shúshí diàn	熟食店
delicious	hǎochī	好吃
democracy	mínzhǔ	民主
demonstration (in street)	yóuxíng	游行
Denmark	Dānmài	丹麦
dentist	yákē yīshēng	牙科医生
dentist's office	yákē zhěnsuǒ	牙科诊所
depart	líkāi	离开
department	bùmén, kē	部门，科
department store	bǎihuò shāngdiàn	百货商店
departure time (planes)	qǐfēi shíjiān	起飞时间
deposit (bank)	chǔxù	储蓄
deposit (pledge)	yājīn	押金
depressed (mood)	qíngxù bù hǎo	情绪不好
dermatologist	pífūkē yīshēng	皮肤科医生
dermatology department	pífūkē	皮肤科
descend	xià	下
descend (planes)	jiàngluò	降落
describe	xíngróng	形容
desert	shāmò	沙漠
design (v)	shèjì	设计
designer	shèjìshī	设计师

designer (name brand)	míngpái	名牌
desk	shūzhuō	书桌
dessert	diǎnxin	点心
detergent	qùwūfěn	去污粉
detour	wānlù	弯路
develop (film)	chōng, chōngxǐ	冲，冲洗
diabetes	tángniàobìng	糖尿病
diagnosis	zhěnduàn	诊断
dial (v)	bō	拨
dialog (theater)	duìbái	对白
diamond	zuànshí	钻石
diaphragm (camera)	guāngquān	光圈
diarrhea	lā dùzi	拉肚子
diced meat or vegetable	dīng	丁
die (v)	sǐ, qùshì	死，去逝
diet (foods eaten)	yīnshí	饮食
diet (weight loss)	jiéshí	节食
dietician	yíngyǎng yīshī	营养医师
different	bù yíyàng	不一样
difficulty	kùnnán	困难
dig	wā	挖
dignified	yǒu qìpài	有气派
diligent	qínfèn	勤奋
dim sum	diǎnxin	点心
dining car	cānchē	餐车
dining room	cāntīng	餐厅
dinner (supper)	wǎnfàn	晚饭
dip (v)	zhàn	蘸
diplomat	wàijiāoguān	外交官
diplomatic	wàijiāo	外交
director (artistic)	dǎoyǎn	导演
director (of an organization)	zhǔrèn	主任
dirty	zāng	脏
disastrous	zāogāo	糟糕
disco	dīsìkē	迪斯科
discomfort	bù shūfu	不舒服
discount (n)	zhékòu	折扣
discover	fāxiàn	发现
discussion	tǎolùn	讨论

DICTIONARY

dish (plate, tray)	*pán*	盘
dishwashing liquid	*xǐdíjì*	洗涤剂
disinfectant	*xiāodú jì*	消毒剂
disk film	*pán shì jiāopiàn*	盘式胶片
disperse	*sàn*	散
distance	*jùlí*	距离
district	*qū*	区
disturb	*dǎrǎo, gānrǎo*	打扰，干扰
divide	*fēn*	分
divorce	*líhūn*	离婚
dizzy	*tóuyūn*	头晕
do (be occupied with)	*zuò*	做
do business	*zuò shēngyì*	做生意
Do not...	*bié, búyào...*	别，不要……
dock (n)	*mǎtóu*	码头
doctor	*yīshēng, dàifu*	医生，大夫
documentary (film)	*jìlù piān*	记录片
doesn't work	*bù xíng*	不行
dog	*gǒu*	狗
dollar	*yuán*	元
domestic (national)	*guónèi*	国内
don't mind (object to)	*bú zàihu*	不在乎
Donald Duck	*Tánglǎoyā*	唐老鸭
door	*mén*	门
door god	*ménshén*	门神
dormitory	*sùshè*	宿舍
double (adj)	*shuāng*	双
double bed	*shuāngrén chuáng*	双人床
double happiness	*shuāngxǐ*	喜
double-sided embroidery	*shuāngmiàn xiù*	双面绣
dough figure	*miànrén*	面人
down	*xià*	下
downstairs	*lóuxià*	楼下
downtown	*shìzhōngxīn*	市中心
dragon	*lóng*	龙
Dragon Well tea	*Lóngjīng chá*	龙井茶
dragon dance	*lóngwǔ*	龙舞
drain (n)	*xiàshuǐdào*	下水道
drama	*xìjù*	戏剧
drawing	*túhuà*	图画
dress rehearsal	*cǎipái*	彩排

dresser	yīchú	衣橱
dressing room	huàzhuāng shì	化装室
dried bean curd	dòufu gān	豆付干
dried shrimps	hǎimǐ	海米
drink	hē	喝
drive (v)	kāichē	开车
driver (bus, taxi)	sījī	司机
driver's license	jiàshǐ zhízhào	驾驶执照
drop (n)	dī	滴
drop (v)	diào	掉
drug	yào	药
drug (narcotic)	dúpǐn	毒品
drugstore	yàodiàn	药店
drum (n)	gǔ	鼓
drum tower	gǔlóu	鼓楼
dry	gān	干
dry clean	gānxǐ	干洗
dry white wine	gān bái pútao jiǔ	干白葡萄酒
dubbed film	yìzhì piān	译制片
duck	yāzi	鸭子
duet (instrumental)	èrchóngzòu	二重奏
duet (vocal)	èrchóngchàng	二重唱
dulcimer	yángqín	扬琴
dull (uninteresting)	dāndiào, méi yìsi	单调,没意思
dumb (mute)	yǎ	哑
dumplings	jiǎozi, bāozi	饺子,包子
duplication machine	fùyìn jī	复印机
during	zài...zhōng	在……中
dustpan	bòji	簸箕
dusty	huīchén duō	灰尘多
dynasty	cháodài	朝代
dysentery	lìji	痢疾
each	měi, měigè	每,每个
each time	měicì	每次
ear	ěrduo	耳朵
ear-nose-throat specialist	ěr-bí-hóu kē dàifu	耳鼻喉科大夫
early	zǎo	早
earn	zhèng	挣
earth (planet)	dìqiú	地球
east	dōng	东

DICTIONARY

East China Sea	Dōnghǎi	东海
easy	róngyì	容易
eat	chī	吃
Economic Daily	Jīngjì Rìbào	经济日报
economics	jīngjìxué	经济学
economy	jīngjì	经济
economy class	pǔtōng cāngwèi	普通舱位
edge	biān	边
editor	biānjì	编辑
education	jiàoyù	教育
eel	shànyú	鳝鱼
effect	xiàoguǒ	效果
efficiency	xiàolǜ	效率
egg	jīdàn	鸡旦
egg-drop soup	dànhuātāng	旦花汤
egg white	dànbái, dànqīng	旦白,旦清
eggplant	qiézi	茄子
Egypt	Āijí	埃及
eight	bā	八
eight precious rice	bābǎofàn	八宝饭
eighty	bāshí	八十
ejaculation	shèjīng	射精
elbow	zhǒu	肘
election	xuǎnjǔ	选举
electrical equipment	diànqì	电器
electricity	diàn	电
electronic	diànzǐ	电子
electrotherapy	diànliáo	电疗
elephant	dàxiàng	大象
elevator	diàntī	电梯
elm tree	yúshù	榆树
embarrassed	bù hǎo yìsi	不好意思
embassy	dàshǐguǎn	大使馆
embroidery	cìxiù	刺绣
emergency	jǐnjí qíngkuàng	紧急情况
emergency room	jízhěn shì	急诊室
emetic	cuītùjì	催吐剂
emperor	huángdì	皇帝
employee	gùyuán	雇员
empress	huánghòu, nǚhuáng	皇后,女皇
empress dowager	tàihòu	太后
empty (adj)	kōng	空

enamel	tángcí	搪瓷
encephalitis	nǎoyán	脑炎
Encore!	Zài lái yí ge!	再来一个！
end (v)	jiéshù	结束
energy (spirit)	jīnglì	精力
engine	fādòngjī	发动机
engineer	gōngchéngshī	工程师
England	Yīngguó	英国
English (language)	Yīngyǔ	英语
engraving	diāokè	雕刻
enjoy	xǐhuan	喜欢
enlargement	fàngdà	放大
enough	zúgòu	足够
ensemble (instrumental)	hézòu	合奏
enter	jìn	进
entrance	rùkǒu, jìnkǒu	入口，进口
entrepreneur	qǐyè jiā	企业家
entry visa	rùjìng qiānzhèng	入境签证
envelope	xìnfēng	信封
episode	chāqǔ	插曲
equal (adj)	píngděng, yíyàng	平等，一样
equal (v)	děngyú	等于
eraser	xiàngpí	橡皮
escalator	zìdòng fútī	自动扶梯
especially	tèbié	特别
et cetera	děng	等
eunuch	tàijiān	太监
Europe	Ōuzhōu	欧洲
even (more)	gèng	更
evening	wǎnshang	晚上
everyday	měitiān	每天
everyone	dàjiā	大家
everything	yíqiè	一切
everywhere	dàochù	到处
evil	huài	坏
example	lìzi	例子
exceed	chāoguò	超过
excellent	fēicháng hǎo	非常好
excellent (slang)	bàng	棒
exchange (ideas)	jiāoliú	交流
exchange (money)	duìhuàn	兑换

123

DICTIONARY

exchange rate	duìhuàn lù	兑换率
exciting	lìngrén jīdòng	令人激动
excuse me (make way)	láojia	劳驾
excuse me (pardon)	duìbuqǐ	对不起
exercise (physical)	duànliàn	锻炼
exhibition	zhǎnlǎn	展览
exit (n)	chūkǒu	出口
exit visa	chūjìng qiānzhèng	出境签证
expectation	qīwàng	期望
expense	fèiyòng	费用
expensive	guì	贵
experience (n)	jīngyàn	经验
experiment	shìyàn	试验
expert	zhuānjiā	专家
expertise	zhuāncháng	专长
explain	jiěshì	解释
export goods	chūkǒu huò	出口货
export license	chūkǒu xǔkě zhèng	出口许可证
express (speed)	tèkuài	特快
express (to convey)	biǎodá	表达
extension (phone)	fēnjī	分机
extension cord	diànxiàn	电线
external use	wàiyòng	外用
extra (surplus)	fùyù de	富余的
extra large	tèdà hào	特大号
extra small	tèxiǎo hào	特小号
extract a tooth	báyá	拔牙
extremely	jí	极
eye (n)	yǎnjing	眼睛
eye drops	yǎn yàoshuǐ	眼药水
face (n)	liǎn	脸
face cream	miànshuāng	面霜
facial (n)	měiróng	美容
factory	gōngchǎng	工厂
Fahrenheit	huáshì	华氏
faint	tóuhūn	头昏
fake	màopái	冒牌
fall (v)	shuāidǎo, diào	摔倒，掉
false	jiǎ de	假的
family	jiā, jiātíng	家，家庭

family members	*jiātíng chéngyuán*	家庭成员
fan, electric	*diànshàn*	电扇
fan, folding	*zhéshàn*	折扇
fan, hand-held	*shànzi*	扇子
Fantastic!	*Juéle!*	绝了！
far	*yuǎn*	远
fare (bus, taxi, or train)	*chēfèi*	车费
farm	*nóngchǎng*	农场
farmer	*nóngmín*	农民
farmer's home	*nóngjiā*	农家
fast (speed)	*kuài*	快
fast food	*kuàicān*	快餐
fat (adj)	*pàng*	胖
fat (n)	*zhīfáng*	脂肪
father	*fùqin*	父亲
faucet	*lóngtóu*	龙头
feature film	*gùshi piān*	故事片
February	*èryuè*	二月
fee	*fèi*	费
feel (sense)	*juéde*	觉得
female (animals)	*cí, mǔ*	雌，母
female (people)	*nǚ*	女
fencing	*jījiàn*	击剑
fertilizer	*féiliào*	肥料
fever	*fāshāo*	发烧
few	*hěnshǎo, bù duō*	很少，不多
fiction	*xiǎoshuō*	小说
fiddle, Beijing opera	*jīnghú*	京胡
fiddle, two-stringed	*èrhú*	二胡
field (farm)	*tián*	田
field (for athletics)	*yùndòng chǎng*	运动场
fifty	*wǔshí*	五十
fig	*wúhuāguǒ*	无花果
fill a tooth	*bǔyá*	补牙
fill in (a form)	*tián*	填
film (for camera)	*jiāojuǎn*	胶卷
film (movie)	*diànyǐng*	电影
film festival	*diànyǐng jié*	电影节
film studio	*diànyǐng chǎng*	电影厂
final (adj)	*zuìhòu*	最后
finally	*zhōngyú*	终于

DICTIONARY

find (v)	zhǎo	找
fine (delicate)	jīngzhì	精致
fine (good)	hěnhǎo, tínghǎo	很好，挺好
fine arts	yìshù	艺术
finger	shǒuzhǐ	手指
fingernail polish	zhǐjia yóu	指甲油
fingernail polish remover	tuìguāng shuǐ	退光水
finish (v)	wánchéng	完成
finished	wán le	完了
Finland	Fēnlán	芬兰
fire (n)	huǒ	火
fire equipment	mièhuǒ qì	灭火器
fire escape	ānquán tī	安全梯
fire exit	tàipíng mén	太平门
fire fighter	xiāofáng duìyuán	消防队员
first (beforehand)	xiān	先
first, the	dìyī	第一
first-aid station	jíjiù zhàn	急救站
first class (seat)	tóuděng cāng	头等舱
first run (bus or train)	shǒu bān chē, tóu bān chē	首班车，头班车
fish	yú	鱼
fisherfolk	yúmín	渔民
fishing	diàoyú	钓鱼
fishing village	yúcūn	渔村
five	wǔ	五
five-grain liquor	wǔliángyè	五粮液
fix (repair)	xiūlǐ	修理
flag (n)	qí	旗
flash (camera)	shǎnguāng dēng	闪光灯
flashlight	shǒudiàntǒng	手电筒
flask	hú	壶
flight (airline)	hángbān	航班
flight schedule	fēixíng shíkèbiǎo	飞行时刻表
floor (of a room)	dìbǎn	地板
floor (story)	céng, lóu	层，楼
flour	miànfěn	面粉
flower	huā	花
flu	liúgǎn	流感
fluent	liúlì	流利
flute, bamboo	dízi	笛子

fly (insect)	*cāngying*	苍蝇
fly (v)	*fēi*	飞
Flying Pigeon (bike)	*Fēigē*	飞鸽
fog	*wù*	雾
folder	*jiāzi*	夹子
folk dance	*mínjiān wǔdǎo*	民间舞蹈
folk music	*mínjiān yīnyuè*	民间音乐
folk tale	*mínjiān gùshì*	民间故事
folklore	*mínjiān chuánshuō*	民间传说
follow	*gēn*	跟
food	*shípǐn, shíwù*	食品,食物
food poisoning	*shíwù zhòng dú*	食物中毒
foot (12 inches)	*yīngchǐ*	英尺
foot (body)	*jiǎo, zú*	脚,足
football (American)	*gǎnlǎnqiú*	橄榄球
footlight	*jiǎodēng*	脚灯
for example	*bǐrú, bǐfang shuō*	比如,比方说
Forbidden City (Palace Museum)	*Gùgōng*	故宫
foreign	*wàiguó*	外国
foreign affairs office	*wàishì bàngōngshì*	外事办公室
foreign exchange certificate	*wàihuìjuàn, wàihuì*	外汇券,外汇
foreign exchange desk	*wàibì duìhuàn tái*	外币兑换台
foreign expert	*wàiguó zhuānjiā*	外国专家
foreign guest	*wàibīn*	外宾
foreign policy	*wàijiāo zhèngcè*	外交政策
foreign student	*liúxuéshēng*	留学生
foreigner	*wàiguórén*	外国人
forest	*sēnlín*	森林
Forever (bike)	*Yǒngjiǔ*	永久
forget	*wàngjì*	忘记
forgive	*yuánliàng*	原谅
fork	*chāzi*	叉子
fork (road)	*chà lùkǒu*	叉路口
form (printed sheet)	*biǎogé*	表格
forty	*sìshí*	四十
forward (sports)	*qiánfēng*	前锋
four	*sì*	四
fox	*húli*	狐狸
fracture	*gǔzhé*	骨折

DICTIONARY

fragile	yìsuì	易碎
fragrant	xiāng	香
franc	fǎláng	法郎
France	Fǎguó	法国
free (no charge)	miǎnfèi	免费
free market	zìyóu shìchǎng	自由市场
freedom	zìyóu	自由
freelancer	zìyóu zhíyè zhě	自由职业者
freeze	dòng	冻
freezing	bīngdòng	冰冻
fresh	xīnxian	新鲜
Friday	xīngqī wǔ	星期五
fried, deep	zhá	炸
fried, lightly	jiān	煎
fried crisp chicken	xiāngsū jī	香酥鸡
fried cruller	yóutiáo	油条
fried dumplings (pot-stickers)	guōtiē	锅贴
fried egg	jiān jīdàn	煎鸡蛋
fried noodles	chǎomiàn	炒面
fried rice	chǎofàn	炒饭
fried sesame twists	máhuā	麻花
friend	péngyǒu	朋友
friendship	yǒuyí	友谊
Friendship Store	Yǒuyí Shāngdiàn	友谊商店
fries, potato	zhá tǔdòu	炸土豆
frog	qīngwā	青蛙
front	qián	前
front door	qiánmén	前门
front section (seating)	qiánpái	前排
front yard	qiányuàn	前院
fruit	shuǐguǒ	水果
fuel	ránliào	燃料
Fuji	Fùshì	富士
full	mǎn	满
full (after meal)	bǎo le	饱了
fun	yǒuqù, hǎowán	有趣,好玩
funny (amusing)	kě xiào, dòu	可笑,逗
fur	qiúpí, pímáo	裘皮,皮毛
furnace	gāolú, lúzi	高炉,炉子
furniture	jiājù	家俱
fuse (n)	bǎoxiǎnsī	保险丝

gallon	jiālún	加仑
game	yóuxì	游戏
game room	yóuyì shì	游艺室
garbage can	lājī xiāng	拉圾箱
garden	huāyuán	花园
garlic	suàn	蒜
gas (coal)	méiqì	煤气
gas (vapor)	qì, qìtǐ	气，气体
gas station	jiāyóu zhàn	加油站
gas stove	méiqìlú	煤气炉
gas tank	yóuxiāng	油箱
gasoline	qìyóu	汽油
gastric	wèi	胃
gastric perforation	wèi chuānkǒng	胃穿孔
gastritis	wèiyán	胃炎
gate	mén	门
gear (driving)	dǎng	档
gear (part)	chǐlún	齿轮
general anesthesia	quánshēn mázuì	全身麻醉
Geneva	Rìnèiwǎ	日内瓦
geranium	xiùqiú	绣球
Germany	Déguó	德国
gesture	dòngzuò	动作
get (obtain)	dé	得
get off (a vehicle)	xiàchē	下车
get off work	xiàbān	下班
get on (a vehicle)	shàng chē	上车
giant panda	dàxióngmāo	大熊猫
gift	lǐwù	礼物
gin (liquor)	dùsōngzǐ jiǔ	杜松子酒
ginger	shēngjiāng	生姜
ginkgo	yínxìng, báiguǒ	银杏，白果
ginkgo tree	báiguǒ shù	白果树
ginseng	rénshēn	人参
girl	nǚhái	女孩
girlfriend	nǚ péngyǒu	女朋友
give	gěi	给
give away	sòngdiào	送掉
give up hope	xièqì	泻气
glass (cup)	bōli bēi	玻璃杯
glasses (optical)	yǎnjìng	眼镜
glassware	bōli zhìpǐn	玻璃制品

DICTIONARY

glaucoma	qīngguāng yǎn	青光眼
glucose	pútáo táng	葡萄糖
glue (mucilage)	jiāoshuǐ	胶水
glue (paste)	jiànghu	浆糊
glutinous rice cake	niángāo	年糕
go (board game)	wéiqí	围棋
go (v)	qù	去
Go! (sports)	Jiā yóu!	加油！
go around (an obstacle)	ràokāi	绕开
goalie (sports)	shǒuményuán	守门员
goat	shānyáng	山羊
gold	jīn	金
golden-haired monkey	jīnsīhóu	金丝猴
goldfish	jīnyú	金鱼
golf	gāo'ěrfū	高尔夫
gong	luó	锣
good	hǎo	好
good luck	hǎo yùnqi	好运气
good morning	zǎochén hǎo	早晨好
good-bye	zàijiàn	再见
good-looking	hǎokàn	好看
goods (stock)	huò	货
goose	é	鹅
gorge	xiá	峡
government	zhèngfǔ	政府
grade school	xiǎoxué	小学
graduate (v)	bìyè	毕业
grain (crop)	liángshi	粮食
grain coupon	liángpiào	粮票
gram	kè	克
grammar	yǔfǎ	语法
Grand Canal	Dàyùnhé	大运河
granddaughter	sūnnǚ, wài sūnnǚ	孙女，外孙女
grandfather (maternal)	lǎoyé, wàigōng	老爷，外公
grandfather (paternal)	yéye	爷爷
grandmother (maternal)	lǎolao, wàipó	姥姥，外婆
grandmother (paternal)	nǎinai	奶奶

grandson	sūnzi, wàisūn	孙子,外孙
grape	pútáo	葡萄
grasp (v)	zhuā	抓
gray	huīsè	灰色
Great!	Zhēn bàng!	真棒!
Great Hall of the People	Rénmín Dàhuìtáng	人民大会堂
Great Wall	Chángchéng	长城
Greece	Xīlà	希腊
green	lǜ	绿
green onion	dàcōng	大葱
green tea	lǜchá	绿茶
greeting card	jìniàn kǎ	纪念卡
grilled	kǎo	烤
groceries	shípǐn	食品
grocery store	shípǐn diàn	食品店
grotto	shíkū	石窟
ground (n)	dì	地
ground meat	ròumò	肉末
group (people)	tuántǐ, qún	团体,群
group visa	jítǐ qiānzhèng	集体签证
grow (plant)	zhòng	种
guarantee	bǎozhèng	保证
guard (sports)	hòuwèi	后卫
guesthouse	bīnguǎn, zhāodàisuǒ	宾馆,招待所
guide (person)	dǎoyóu	导游
guidebook	dǎoyóu shū	导游书
guitar	jíta	吉他
guitar, 3-string	sānxián qín	三弦琴
gun	qiāng	枪
gymnasium	tǐyùguǎn	体育馆
gymnastics	tǐcāo	体操
gynecologist	fùkē yīshēng	妇科医生
gynecology department	fùkē	妇科
habit (custom)	xíguàn	习惯
hair	tóufa	头发
hair oil	fàyóu	发油
hairbrush	tóushuā	头刷
haircut	lǐfà	理发
hairspray	dìngxíng yè	定型液

DICTIONARY

half	yíbàn, bàngè	一半，半个
half a day	bàntiān	半天
half-price	bànjià	半价
halt	zhànzhù	站住
ham	huǒtuǐ	火腿
hammer	chuízi	锤子
hand (n)	shǒu	手
hand carry-on	suíshēn xínglǐ	随身行李
hand towel	shǒujīn	手巾
hand wash	shǒu xǐ	手洗
handball	shǒuqiú	手球
handicapped person	cánjí rén	残疾人
handicraft	shǒugōngyì pǐn	手工艺品
handkerchief	shǒujuàn	手绢
handlebar (bike)	chēbǎ	车把
handmade	shǒugōng zhìzuò	手工制作
happen	fāshēng	发生
happiness	xìngfú	幸福
happiness (symbol)	xǐ	喜
harbor	gǎng	港
hard-seat	yìngzuò	硬座
hard-sleeper	yìngwò	硬卧
harvest (n)	shōuhuò	收获
hat	màozi	帽子
hate	hèn	恨
have	yǒu	有
haw	shānzhā	山楂
Hawaii	Xiàwēiyí	夏威夷
hay fever	huāfěn rè	花粉热
he	tā	他
head	tóu	头
headache	tóuténg	头疼
headlight	qiándēng	前灯
health	jiànkāng	健康
health care	bǎojiàn	保健
health club	jiànshēn fáng	健身房
health declaration	jiànkāng biǎo	健康表
heart	xīnzàng, xīn	心脏，心
heart attack	xīnzàngbìng fāzuò	心脏病发作
heat (energy)	rèliàng, rè	热量，热
heat (radiator)	nuǎnqì	暖气
heat (v)	jiārè	加热

heavy	chén, zhòng	沉，重
heavy (taste)	nóng	浓
hectare	gōngqīng	公顷
hedge rose	qiángwēi	蔷薇
height	gāodù	高度
hello	nǐhǎo	你好
help (n)	bāngzhù	帮助
help (v)	bāng	帮
Helsinki	Hè'ěrxīnjī	赫尔辛基
hemorrhage	chūxuè	出血
Henan Opera	yùjù	豫剧
hepatitis	gānyán	肝炎
her	tāde	她的
herbal medicine	cǎoyào	草药
here	zhèlǐ, zhèr	这里，这儿
hero	yīngxióng	英雄
heroin	hǎiluòyīn	海洛因
heroine	nǚ yīngxióng	女英雄
hesitation	yóuyù	犹豫
hey	wèi	喂
high	gāo	高
high school	zhōngxué	中学
highest	zuìgāo	最高
highland	gāoyuán	高原
highway	gōnglù	公路
hill	shān	山
Hilton	Xī'ěrdùn	希尔顿
Himalayas	Xīmǎlāyǎ shān	喜玛拉雅山
hip	kuà	胯
hire (a person)	gù	雇
hire (charter)	bāo	包
hired car	bāochē	包车
his	tāde	他的
history	lìshǐ	历史
history museum	lìshǐ bówùguǎn	历史博物馆
hold (embrace)	bào	抱
hold (take)	ná	拿
holder	jiàzi	架子
holiday	jiérì	节日
Holland	Hélán	荷兰
Hollywood	Hǎoláiwū	好莱坞
home	jiā	家

DICTIONARY

home-style	*jiācháng*	家常
homemaker	*zhǔfù*	主妇
Honda	*Běntián*	本田
honey crystalized apples	*básī píngguǒ*	拔丝苹果
Hong Kong	*Xiānggǎng*	香港
Hong Kong dollar	*gǎngbì*	港币
honor	*róngxìng*	荣幸
hook (n)	*gōuzi*	钩子
hope	*xīwàng*	希望
horrible	*kěpà*	可怕
hors d'oeuvre	*lěngpán*	冷盘
horse	*mǎ*	马
hospital	*yīyuàn*	医院
hospitality	*hàokè, zhāodài*	好客，招待
host (person)	*zhǔrén*	主人
host organization	*jiēdài dānwèi*	接待单位
hostel	*lǚshè*	旅社
hot	*rè*	热
hot (spicy)	*là*	辣
hot-and-sour soup	*suānlà tāng*	酸辣汤
hot pot	*huǒguō*	火锅
hot sauce	*làjiàng*	辣酱
hot spring	*wēnquán*	温泉
hot water (from tap)	*rèshuǐ*	热水
hotel	*lǚguǎn, fàndiàn*	旅馆，饭店
hour	*xiǎoshí*	小时
house	*fángzi*	房子
housekeeping department	*kèfáng bù*	客房部
how	*zěnme*	怎么
how far	*duōyuǎn*	多远
how long (length)	*duōcháng*	多长
how long (time)	*duōjiǔ*	多久
how many	*jǐ gè, duōshao*	几个，多少
how much	*duōshao*	多少
how old (person)	*duōdà*	多大
humid	*cháoshī*	潮湿
humor	*yōumò*	幽默
humor, sense of	*yōumò gǎn*	幽默感
hundred	*bǎi*	百
hundred million	*yì*	亿

hunting	dǎliè	打猎
hurry up	gǎnkuài	赶快
hurt	téng	疼
husband	zhàngfu, àirén	丈夫，爱人
Hyatt	Kǎiyuè	凯乐
hypertension	gāo xuèyā	高血压
hypodermic	píxià	皮下
hypotension	dī xuèyā	低血压
I	wǒ	我
ice	bīng	冰
ice cream	bīngqílín	冰淇淋
ice hockey	bīngqiú	冰球
ice water	bīngshuǐ	冰水
idea	zhúyì, xiǎngfǎ	主意，想法
idiom	chéngyǔ	成语
if	rúguǒ	如果
illness	bìng	病
image	xíngxiàng	形象
imitate	mófǎng	模仿
immediately	mǎshàng	马上
immigrant	yímín	移民
immigration checkpoint	yímín jiǎnchá zhàn	移民检查站
implement (a policy)	zhíxíng	执行
import	jìnkǒu	进口
import goods	jìnkǒu huò	进口货
import license	jìnkǒu xǔkězhèng	进口许可证
important	zhòngyào	重要
impression (thought)	yìnxiàng	印象
inch (n)	yīngcùn	英寸
increase	zēngjiā	增加
India	Yìndù	印度
indigestion	xiāohuà bù liáng	消化不良
individual	gèrén, gètǐ	个人，个体
industry	gōngyè, chǎnyè	工业，产业
inexpensive	búguì	不贵
infection	fāyán	发炎
infectious	chuánrǎn	传染
inflammation	fāyán	发炎
information (knowledge)	zhīshì	知识

DICTIONARY

information (news)	xiāoxi	消息
information desk	wènxùn chù	问询处
injection	zhùshè, dǎzhēn	注射,打针
ink (for calligraphy)	mòzhī	墨汁
ink (for fountain pen)	mòshuǐ	墨水
ink painting, Chinese	shuǐmò huà	水墨画
ink slab	yàntai	砚台
ink stick	mò	墨
Inner Mongolia	Nèiměnggǔ	内蒙古
inpatient department	zhùyuàn chù	住院处
inquire	xúnwèn	询问
insect	kūnchóng	昆虫
inside	lǐ	里
insignia (badge)	huīzhāng	徽章
insomnia	shīmián	失眠
instrumental music	qìyuè	器乐
insure	bǎoxiǎn	保险
intellectual	zhīshì fènzǐ	知识分子
intelligent	cōngming	聪明
interesting	yǒu yìsi	有意思
intermission	mùjiān xiūxi	幕间休息
intern	shíxí shēng	实习生
internal	nèi	内
international	guójì	国际
interpreter	fānyì	翻译
intersection (crossroad)	shízì lùkǒu	十字路口
intravenous injection	jìngmài zhùshè	静脉注射
introduction	jièshào	介绍
inventor	fāmíngzhě	发明者
investigate	diàochá	调查
invitation card	qǐngtiě	请帖
iron (for clothing)	yùndǒu	熨斗
iron (metal)	tiě	铁
iron (v)	yùn, tàng	熨,烫
Iron Goddess of Mercy tea	Tiěguānyīn chá	铁观音茶
iron openwork	tiěhuā	铁花
is	shì	是
isolation ward	gélí bìngfáng	隔离病房
it	tā	它
It's a pity	hěn yíhàn	很遗憾

It's nothing	*méi guānxi*	没关系
Italian opera	*Yìdàlì gējù*	意大利歌剧
Italy	*Yìdàlì*	意大利
itch	*yǎng*	痒
itinerary	*rìchéng*	日程
ivory	*xiàngyá*	象牙
ivory carving	*yádiāo*	牙雕
jacket	*jiākè*	夹克
jade	*yù*	玉
jade carving	*yùdiāo*	玉雕
jade carving factory	*yùdiāo chǎng*	玉雕厂
jail	*jiānyù*	监狱
jam (jelly)	*guǒjiàng*	果酱
January	*yīyuè*	一月
Japan	*Rìběn*	日本
Japanese yen	*rìyuán*	日元
jar	*píng, guàn*	瓶，罐
jasmine tea	*mòlì huāchá*	茉莉花茶
jaw	*xiàba*	下巴
jaywalking	*luàn chuān mǎlù*	乱穿马路
jazz music	*juéshìyuè*	爵士乐
jeep	*jípǔchē*	吉普车
jellyfish	*hǎizhé*	海蜇
jetlag	*shíchā fǎnying*	时差反应
jewel (precious)	*zhūbǎo*	珠宝
jewelry (ornamental)	*shǒushì*	首饰
job	*gōngzuò*	工作
join	*cānjiā*	参加
joints (body)	*guānjié*	关节
joke (v)	*kāi wánxiào*	开玩笑
journal (diary)	*rìjì*	日记
journal (periodical)	*qīkān, kānwù*	期刊，刊物
journalism	*xīnwén gōngzuò*	新闻工作
journalist (reporter)	*jìzhě*	记者
judge (n)	*fǎguān*	法官
judge (v)	*pànduàn*	判断
judo	*róudào*	柔道
juice (fruit)	*guǒzhī*	果汁
July	*qīyuè*	七月
jump	*tiào, bèng*	跳，蹦
jumprope (n)	*tiàoshéng*	跳绳
June	*liùyuè*	六月

DICTIONARY

just	jiù	就
just now	cái, gāngcái	才, 刚才
karst	yánróng	岩溶
Keemun tea	Qímén hóngchá	祁门红茶
keep	bǎoliú	保留
ketchup (catsup)	fānqié jiàng	蕃茄酱
key (n)	yàoshi	钥匙
keyboard instrument	jiànpán yuèqì	键盘乐器
kick (v)	tī	踢
kidney	shèn	肾
kidney bean	yúndòu	云豆
kidskin	xiǎoshānyáng pí	小山羊皮
Kiev	Jīfǔ	基辅
kill (v)	shā	杀
kilogram	gōngjīn	公斤
kilometer	gōnglǐ	公里
kind (personality)	shànliáng	善良
kindergarten	yòu'éryuán	幼儿园
kiss (n)	qīn, wěn	亲, 吻
kitchen	chúfáng	厨房
kite	fēngzheng	风筝
knee	xīgài	膝盖
knife	dāozi	刀子
knit	zhī	织
know (a fact)	zhīdao	知道
know (a person)	rènshì	认识
know how to	huì	会
knowledge	zhīshì	知识
Kodak	Kēdá	柯达
Korea	Cháoxiǎn	朝鲜
Kowloon	Jiǔlóng	九龙
Kublai Khan	Hūbìliè	忽必烈
kumquat	jīnjú	金桔
Kunshan Opera	kūnqǔ	昆曲
Kyoto	Jīngdū	京都
label (n)	biāoqiān	标签
labor union	gōnghuì	工会
laboratory	huàyàn shì	化验室
lacquer, carved	diāoqī	雕漆
lacquerware	qīqì	漆器
lake	hú	湖

lamasery	lǎmàsì	喇嘛寺
lamb (mutton)	yángròu	羊肉
lambskin	xiǎoyáng pí	小羊皮
lamp	dēng	灯
land (earth)	tǔdì	土地
landscape	fēngjǐng	风景
lane	hútong, xiàng	胡同,巷
language	yǔyán	语言
large	dà	大
largest	zuìdà	最大
last (final)	zuìhòu	最后
last month	shàng ge yuè	上个月
last one	zuìhòu yígè	最后一个
last run (bus or train)	mòbān chē	末班车
last week	shàng ge xīngqī	上个星期
last year	qùnián	去年
later (afterwards)	hòulái	后来
later (in a while)	yìhuìr	一会儿
laundry (clean)	xǐ wán de yīfu	洗完的衣服
laundry (dirty)	yào xǐ de yīfu	要洗的衣服
laundry bag	xǐyīdài	洗衣袋
laundry detergent	xǐyīfěn	洗衣粉
law	fǎlù	法律
lawyer	lùshī	律师
layered	duōcéng	多层
lazy	lǎn	懒
lead (v)	dài, lǐng	带,领
lead actor (or actress)	zhǔyǎn	主演
leader	lǐngdǎo	领导
leads to (street)	tōngxiàng	通向
leaf	shùyè	树叶
leak (v)	lòu	漏
lean (thin)	shòu	瘦
leapord	bào	豹
learn	xué	学
leather	pígé	皮革
leather shoes	píxié	皮鞋
leave (behind)	liú	留
leave (depart)	líkāi	离开
leave (set out)	chūfā	出发
leave a message (spoken)	liú huà	留话

DICTIONARY

leave a note	liú tiáo	留条
lecture (n)	jiǎngzuò	讲座
left (direction)	zuǒ	左
leg	tuǐ	腿
lemon	níngméng	柠檬
lemonade	níngméng shuǐ	柠檬水
length	chángdù	长度
Leningrad	Lièníngélē	列宁格勒
lens (camera)	jìngtóu	镜头
less	shǎo	少
lesser panda	xiǎoxióngmāo	小熊猫
lesson (class)	kè	课
lesson (moral)	jiàoxùn	教训
let	ràng	让
letter (mail)	xìn	信
lettuce	wōjù	莴苣
level (degree)	shuǐpíng	水平
Li River	Líjiāng	漓江
liberalism	zìyóuhuà	自由化
library	túshūguǎn	图书馆
license plate	chēpái	车牌
lie down	tǎng xià	躺下
life	shēnghuó	生活
light (in color, density)	qiǎn, dàn	浅，淡
light (lamp)	dēng	灯
light (to kindle)	diǎn	点
light (weight)	qīng	轻
light meter	cèguāng biǎo	测光表
lighting	zhàomíng	照明
lighting design	dēngguāng shèjì	灯光设计
like (v)	xǐhuan	喜欢
like this (this way)	zhèyàng	这样
lilac	dīngxiāng	丁香
line (n)	xiàn	线
linen	yàmá bù	亚麻布
linguistics	yǔyánxué	语言学
lion	shīzi	狮子
lion dance	shīzi wǔ	狮子舞
liquor	jiǔ	酒
lira	lǐlā	里拉
listen to	tīng	听

listen to music	tīng yīnyuè	听音乐
liter	shēng	升
literature	wénxué	文学
lithograph	shíbǎnhuà	石版画
little (small)	xiǎo	小
live (reside)	zhù	住
live telecast	xiànchǎng zhíbō	现场直播
liver	gān	肝
living	huózhe	活着
living room	kètīng	客厅
lobby (n)	xiūxìshì	休息室
lobster	lóngxiā	龙虾
local (place)	dìfāng	地方
local (slow bus or train)	mànchē	慢车
local (within a city)	běndì, dāngdì	本地，当地
local anesthesia	júbù mázuì	局部麻醉
local guide	dìpéi	地陪
local money, Chinese	rénmínbì	人民币
local opera	dìfāng xì	地方戏
located at	zài	在
location	dìdiǎn	地点
lock	suǒ	锁
lock (ship)	chuánzhá	船闸
locust tree	huáishù	槐树
London	Lúndūn	伦敦
lonely	jìmò	寂寞
long (adj)	cháng	长
long bean, green	jiāngdòu	江豆
long-distance	chángtú	长途
long-distance bus	chángtú qìchē	长途汽车
long live...	...wànsuì	…万岁
longan fruit	lóngyǎn	龙眼
longevity	chángshòu	长寿
longevity (symbol)	shòu	寿
look	kàn	看
loose	sōngsǎn	松散
loquat	pípā	枇杷
Los Angeles	Luòshānjī	洛杉矶
lose	diūshī	丢失
lost (an object)	diū le	丢了
lost (the way)	mílù	迷路

DICTIONARY

lost-and-found office	shīwù zhāolǐng chù	失物领招处
lotus flower	liánhuā, héhuā	莲花,荷花
lotus root	ǒu	藕
lotus seed	liánzǐ	莲子
loud	dàshēng	大声
love (n)	àiqíng	爱情
love (v)	ài	爱
low	dī	低
lowest	zuìdī	最低
luck	yùnqi	运气
luck (symbol)	fú	福
luggage (see baggage)	xíngli	行李
luggage rack	xíngli jià	行李架
lumbago	yāoténg	腰疼
lunch (n)	wǔfàn	午饭
lung	fèi	肺
lute, 4-string	pípá	琵琶
lychee (litchi)	lìzhī	荔枝
lynx	shēli	猞猁
lyrics (song)	gēcí	歌词
Macao	Àomén	澳门
machine	jīqì	机器
Madrid	Mǎdélǐ	马德里
magazine (reading)	zázhì	杂志
magic	móshù	魔术
magician	móshùshī	魔术师
mah-jongg	májiàng	麻将
mail (letters)	xìn	信
mail (v)	jì	寄
mailbox	yóutǒng	邮筒
main	zhǔyào	主要
main character	zhǔjué	主角
main desk	zǒngtái	总台
maitre d'	zǒngguǎn	总管
make	zuò	做
make progress	yǒu jìnzhǎn	有进展
make-up (cosmetics)	huàzhuāng	化妆
malaria	nüèjí	疟疾
male (animals)	gōng, xióng	公,雄
male (people)	nán	男

man	nánrén	男人
management	guǎnlǐ	管理
manager	jīnglǐ	经理
Manchurian jasper	xiùyù	岫玉
mandarin ducks	yuānyang	鸳鸯
mandarin orange	gānzi	柑子
mandolin, 4-string	yuèqín	月琴
mango	mángguǒ	芒果
manicure	xiū zhǐjia	修指甲
manual transmission (car)	shǒudòng huàndǎng	手动换档
manufacture (produce)	shēngchǎn	生产
many	hǎo duō	好多
Mao cap	jūnmào	军帽
Mao jacket	jūnbiànfú	军便服
Maotai liquor	máotái	茅台
map (n)	dìtú	地图
marble	dàlǐshí	大理石
March	sānyuè	三月
Marco Polo	Mǎkě Bōluó	马可·波罗
marijuana	dàmá	大麻
marine (military)	hǎijūn lùzhànduì	海军陆战队
marionette	tíxiàn mù'ǒu	提线木偶
mark (currency)	mǎkè	马克
marriage	hūnyīn	婚姻
marry	jiéhūn	结婚
marten	diāo	貂
martial arts	wǔshù	武术
martial arts performer	wǔshù biǎoyǎnzhě	武术表演者
martyr	lièshì	烈士
mashed potatos	tǔdòu ní	土豆泥
mask	miànjù	面具
massage	ànmó, tuīná	按摩,推拿
masses (people)	qúnzhòng	群众
master worker	shīfu	师傅
matches	huǒchái	火柴
maternity ward	chǎnkē bìngfáng	产科病房
mathematics	shùxué	数学
matter (affair)	shìqing	事情

DICTIONARY

mausoleum	líng	陵
Maxwell House	Màishì	麦氏
May	wǔyuè	五月
maybe	yěxǔ	也许
me	wǒ	我
meaning	yìsi	意思
measles	mázhěn	麻疹
measure (v)	cèliáng	测量
meatball	ròu wánzi	肉丸子
medical science	yīxué	医学
medicine	yīyào	医药
medicine, traditional Chinese	zhōngyào	中药
medium (size)	zhōng hào	中号
meet (a person)	jiàn	见
meeting (n)	huì	会
Melbourne	Mò'ěrběn	墨尔本
melon, Hami	hāmìguā	哈蜜瓜
member (of a group)	chéngyuán	成员
memorial arch	páilóu	牌楼
memorial hall	jìniàntáng	纪念堂
memory	jìyì	记忆
men's bike	nánchē	男车
mend	bǔ	补
meningitis	nǎomó yán	脑膜炎
menstruation	yuèjīng	月经
mental	jīngshén	精神
menu	càidān	菜单
Mercedes Benz	Bēnchí	奔驰
merchandise	shāngpǐn	商品
metal	jīnshǔ	金属
meter (metric)	mǐ	米
meter (taxi)	jìjiàqì	计价器
method	fāngfǎ	方法
metric ton	gōngdūn	公吨
Mickey Mouse	Mǐlǎoshǔ	米老鼠
microphone	huàtǒng	话筒
midnight	bànyè	半夜
mile	yīnglǐ	英里
military	jūnshì	军事
military band	jūnyuèduì	军乐队

milk	niúnǎi	牛奶
Milky Way	Yínhé	银河
milliliter	háoshēng	毫升
millimeter	háomǐ	毫米
million	bǎiwàn	百万
mind (brain)	tóunǎo	头脑
mine (my)	wǒde	我的
mineral water	kuàngquán shuǐ	矿泉水
Ming Tombs	Shísānlíng	十三陵
mini-bus	miànbāochē	面包车
miniature bottle painting	bíyānhú	鼻烟壶
miniature carving	wēidiāo	微雕
mink	shuǐdiāo	水貂
Minolta	Měinéngdá	美能达
minorities' dance	mínzú wǔdǎo	民族舞蹈
minority nationality	shǎoshù mínzú	少数民族
minute (n)	fēnzhōng	分钟
mirror (n)	jìngzi	镜子
miscellaneous	záwù, záshì	杂务，杂事
mischievous	táoqì	淘气
Miss	xiǎojiě	小姐
mistake (n)	cuòwù	错误
mistake (v)	nòngcuò, gǎocuò	弄错，搞错
Mitsubishi	Sānlíng	三菱
model (of an object)	móxíng	模型
model (person)	mótèr	模特儿
modern (advanced)	xiàndài	现代
modern (style)	xiàndàipài	现代派
modernization	xiàndàihuà	现代化
monastery	sì, sìyuàn	寺，寺院
Monday	xīngqī yī	星期一
money	qián	钱
money order	huìpiào	汇票
Mongolian hot pot	shuànyángròu	涮羊肉
monk	héshàng	和尚
monkey	hóuzi	猴子
monster	móguǐ, guàiwù	魔鬼，怪物
month	yuè	月
monthly ticket (bus, subway)	yuèpiào	月票

monument	jìniànbēi	纪念碑
moon	yuèliang, yuè	月亮，月
mop (n)	tuōbǎ	拖把
mop (v)	tuōdì	拖地
more	duō	多
morning	zǎochen, shàngwǔ	早晨，上午
morphine	mǎfēi	吗啡
Moscow	Mòsīkē	莫斯科
Moslem	qīngzhēn	清真
mosque	qīngzhēn sì	清真寺
mosquito	wénzi	蚊子
most (comparative)	zuì	最
most (majority of)	dà duōshù	大多数
mother	mǔqīn	母亲
motor	mǎdá	马达
Mount Everest	Zhūmùlángmǎ fēng	珠穆朗玛峰
mountain	shān	山
mountaineering	dēngshān	登山
mounting	zhuāngbiǎo	装裱
mouth	zuǐ	嘴
mouth organ, Chinese	shēng	笙
mouthwash	shùkǒu jì	漱口剂
move aside (objects)	bānkāi	搬开
move aside (people)	ràngkāi	让开
movement (music)	yuèzhāng	乐章
movie	diànyǐng	电影
movie camera	diànyǐng shèxiàngjī	电影摄像机
movie star	yǐngxīng	影星
Mr.	xiānsheng	先生
Mrs.	tàitai, fūrén	太太，夫人
Ms.	nǚshì	女士
MSG	wèijīng	味精
much	duō	多
mug	bēizi	杯子
mulberry tree	sāngshù	桑树
multiply	chéng	乘
mung bean	lǜdòu	绿豆
mural	bìhuà	壁画
muscle	jīròu	肌肉
museum	bówùguǎn	博物馆

mushroom	*mógu*	蘑菇
music	*yīnyuè*	音乐
musical (show)	*gēwǔ jù*	歌舞剧
musical instrument	*yuèqì*	乐器
musical staff, 5-line	*wǔxiàn pǔ*	五线谱
must	*bìxū*	必须
mustard (condiment)	*jièmo*	芥末
mustard, leaf	*gàicài*	芥菜
musty	*fāméi*	发霉
mutton	*yángròu*	羊肉
my	*wǒde*	我的
My God!	*Wǒde tiān!*	我的天！
nail (hardware)	*dīngzi*	钉子
name (n)	*míngzi*	名字
napkin, paper	*cānjīn zhǐ*	餐巾纸
narcissus	*shuǐxiān*	水仙
narrow	*xiázhǎi*	狭窄
nasal congestion	*bízi bù tōng*	鼻子不通
national (adj)	*guójiā*	国家
national anthem	*guógē*	国歌
national defense	*guófáng*	国防
national emblem	*guóhuī*	国徽
national flag	*guóqí*	国旗
national guide	*quánpéi*	全陪
nationality (ethnic)	*mínzú*	民族
native place (ancestral)	*lǎojiā*	老家
natural	*zìrán*	自然
nature (character)	*xìnggé*	性格
nature (outdoors)	*dà zìrán*	大自然
nauseous	*ěxīn*	恶心
navy	*hǎijūn*	海军
near	*jìn*	近
nearest	*zuìjìn*	最近
neck	*bózi*	脖子
necklace	*xiàngliàn*	项链
need	*xūyào, yào*	需要，要
needle	*zhēn*	针
needle and thread	*zhēnxiàn*	针线
needlework	*zhēnxiàn huó*	针线活

DICTIONARY

negative (film)	dǐpiàn	底片
neighbor	línjū	邻居
Neolithic era	xīn shíqì shídài	新石器时代
Nepal	Níbó'ěr	尼泊尔
nerve	shénjīng	神经
nervous (mood)	jǐnzhāng	紧张
Nescafe	Quècáo	雀巢
neurology	shénjīng bìngxué	神经病学
neurosis	shénjīngzhì	神经质
never	yǒng bù	永不
never again	zài yě bù	再也不
never have	cóng méi	从没
new	xīn	新
New Wave	xīncháo	新潮
New Year	xīnnián, yuándàn	新年，元旦
New Year painting	niánhuà	年画
New York	Niǔyuē	纽约
New Zealand	Xīnxīlán	新西兰
New Zealand dollar	Xīnxīlán yuán	新西兰元
news	xīnwén, xiāoxi	新闻，消息
news program	xīnwén jiémù	新闻节目
newspaper	bàozhǐ	报纸
newsstand	bàotíng, bàotān	报亭，报摊
next (forthcoming)	xiàyígè, xiàmiàn de	下一个，下面的
next stop	xiàzhàn	下站
next time	xià cì	下次
next to (at the side of)	zài...pángbiān	在……旁边
next year	míngnián	明年
nice	hǎo, bú cuò	好，不错
night	yèwǎn	夜晚
night bus	yèbān chē	夜班车
night market	yèshì	夜市
night shift	yèbān	夜班
nightlife	yè shēnghuó	夜生活
nightstand	chuángtóuguì	床头柜
Nikon	Níkāng	尼康
nine	jiǔ	九
ninety	jiǔshí	九十
Nissan	Nísāng	尼桑
noisy	chǎo	吵
nonstaple food	fùshí pǐn	副食品
noodles	miàntiáo	面条

noon	zhōngwǔ	中午
north	běi	北
North America	Běiměizhōu	北美洲
North Pole	Běijí	北极
North Star	Běijí xīng	北极星
nose	bízi	鼻子
not	bù, méi	不，没
not bad	bú cuò	不错
novel (n)	xiǎoshuō	小说
November	shíyīyuè	十一月
now	xiànzài	现在
nuclear	hé	核
numb	má	麻
number (numeral)	hàomǎ	号码
number (quantity)	shùzì	数字
nurse (n)	hùshì	护士
nursery school	tuō'érsuǒ	托儿所
o'clock	diǎnzhōng	点钟
oatmeal	màipiàn	麦片
object (thing)	dōngxi	东西
observation ward	guānchá shì	观察室
ocean	hǎiyáng	海洋
October	shíyuè	十月
of course	dāngrán	当然
office	bàngōngshì	办公室
often	jīngcháng	经常
Oh well (forget it)	suànle	算了
oil	yóu	油
oil (petroleum)	shíyóu	石油
oil painting	yóuhuà	油画
ointment	ruǎngāo	软膏
okay	xíng	行
old (aged)	lǎo	老
old (used)	jiù	旧
old age	lǎonián	老年
old man	lǎo dàye	老大爷
old town (section of a city)	lǎochéng, jiùchéng	老城，旧城
oleander	jiāzhútáo	夹竹桃
olive	gǎnlǎn	橄榄
Olympic Games	Àoyùnhuì	奥运会

DICTIONARY

omelet	dànjiǎo	蛋饺
one	yī	一
one-child policy	dúshēng zǐnǔ zhèngcè	独生子女政策
one-way street	dānxíng xiàn	单行线
one-way ticket	dānchéng piào	单程票
onion	cōngtóu	葱头
only	zhǐ	只
oolong tea	wūlóng chá	乌龙茶
open	kāi	开
open-dated ticket	bú dìngqī piào	不定期票
open for business	kāimén	开门
opera	gējù	歌剧
opera mask	xìjù liǎnpǔ	戏剧脸谱
opera singer (Chinese opera)	xìjù yǎnyuán	戏剧演员
opera singer (Western opera)	gējù yǎnyuán	歌剧演员
operation room	shǒushù shì	手术室
operator (phone)	zǒngjī	总机
ophthamologist	yǎnkē yīshēng	眼科医生
ophthamology department	yǎnkē	眼科
opinion	yìjiàn	意见
opium	yāpiàn	鸦片
opportunity	jīhuì	机会
or	huòzhě, háishì	或者，还是
orange (color)	júhuáng	桔黄
orange (fruit)	gānjú, guǎnggān	柑桔，广柑
orange juice	júzi zhī	桔子汁
orange soda	júzi shuǐ	桔子水
orchestra	jiāoxiǎng yuèduì	交响乐队
orchestra, traditional Chinese	mínzú yuèduì	民族乐队
orchid	lánhuā	兰花
order (command)	mìnglìng	命令
order (for purchase)	dìnggòu	订购
order (sequence)	cìxù	次序
order food	diǎncài	点菜
original (n)	yuánzuò, yuánjiàn	原作，原件
ornament	zhuāngshì	装饰
other	biéde	别的
otter	shuǐtǎ	水獭

ounce	àngsī	盎司
our	wǒmende	我们的
outlet (electrical)	chāzuò	插座
outside	wài	外
outstanding	chūsè	出色
overcoat	dàyī	大衣
overpass	tiānqiáo	天桥
overseas Chinese	Huáqiáo	华侨
overseas edition	hǎiwài bǎn	海外版
overture (music)	xùqǔ	序曲
overworked (tired)	láolèi	劳累
owe	qiàn	欠
own	yǒu	有
ox	niú	牛
oxygen	yǎngqì	氧气
oyster	háo	蚝
oyster sauce	háoyóu	蚝油
Pacific Ocean	Tàipíngyáng	太平洋
pack (v)	zhuāng	装
pack suitcases	dǎ xínglǐ	打行李
package (n)	bāoguǒ	包裹
packaging tape	mìfēng jiāodài	密封胶带
pagoda	tǎ	塔
paid	yǐfù	已付
pain (physical)	téng	疼
pain-killer	zhǐténg yào	止疼药
paint (a picture)	huàhuà	画画
painter (artist)	huàjiā	画家
painting (art)	huìhuà	绘画
painting, traditional Chinese	guóhuà	国画
pajama	shuìyī	睡衣
palace	gōngdiàn	宫殿
palpitation	xīntiào	心跳
pancake (for Peking Duck)	báobǐng	薄饼
panda	xióngmāo	熊猫
pantomime	yǎjù	哑剧
pants	kùzi	裤子
paper	zhǐ	纸
paper clip	zhǐjiā	纸夹

DICTIONARY

papercut (folk art)	jiǎnzhǐ	剪纸
parade (military)	yuèbīng	阅兵
parasol tree, Chinese	wútóngshù	梧桐树
parcel	bāoguǒ	包裹
pardon (an offense)	ráoshù	饶恕
parents	fùmǔ	父母
Paris	Bālí	巴黎
park (a vehicle)	tíng	停
park, public	gōngyuán	公园
parking lot (bikes)	cúnchē chù	存车处
part (not whole)	bùfen	部分
partner	huǒbàn	伙伴
party (gathering)	jùhuì	聚会
party (political)	dǎng	党
party member	dǎngyuán	党员
pass (go beyond)	guò	过
passion	gǎnqíng	感情
passport	hùzhào	护照
past, in the	guòqù	过去
patience	nàixīn	耐心
patient (sick person)	bìngrén	病人
pattern (decorative)	tú'àn	图案
pattern (standard)	guīgé	规格
pavilion	tíngzi	亭子
pay (v)	fùqián	付钱
pea	wāndòu	豌豆
pea-flour cake	wāndòuhuáng	豌豆黄
peace	hépíng	和平
peach	táozi	桃子
peanut	huāshēng	花生
pear	lí	梨
pearl	zhēnzhū	珍珠
pearl cream	zhēnzhū shuāng	珍珠霜
Pearl River	Zhūjiāng	珠江
peasant	nóngmín	农民
pedal (n)	jiǎotàbǎn	脚踏板
peddler	xiǎofàn	小贩
pedestrian	xíngrén	行人
pediatrician	érkē yīshēng	儿科医生
pediatrics department	érkē	儿科
peel (n)	pí	皮

peel (v)	*xiāopí*	削皮
Peking duck	*Běijīng kǎoyā*	北京烤鸭
pen (ball-point)	*yuánzhūbǐ*	圆珠笔
pen (fountain)	*gāngbǐ*	钢笔
pencil	*qiānbǐ*	铅笔
penicillin	*qīngméisù*	青霉素
peony	*mǔdān*	牡丹
people (of a nation)	*rénmín*	人民
People's Daily	*Rénmín Rìbào*	人民日报
pepper (ground)	*hújiāo fěn*	胡椒粉
pepper, green	*qīngjiāo*	青椒
pepper, hot	*làjiāo*	辣椒
percent	*bǎi fēn zhi...*	百分之……
percussion instrument	*dǎjī yuèqì*	打击乐器
performer	*biǎoyǎnzhě*	表演者
perhaps	*yěxǔ*	也许
permanent wave	*tàngfà*	烫发
permission	*xǔkě, yǔnxu*	许可，允许
persimmon	*shìzi*	柿子
person	*rén*	人
person-to-person (phone)	*jiàorén*	叫人
personal effects	*sīrén cáichǎn*	私人财产
personality	*xìnggé*	性格
petroleum	*shíyóu*	石油
Peugeot	*Báirú*	白茹
pharmacist	*yàojì shī*	药剂师
pharmacy	*yàofáng*	药房
Philadelphia	*Fèichéng*	费城
Philippines	*Fēilǜbīn*	菲律宾
phoenix	*fènghuáng*	凤凰
phone (see telephone)	*diànhuà*	电话
photo album	*yīngjí, xiàngcè*	影集，像册
photograph (n)	*zhàopiàn*	照片
photograph (v)	*zhàoxiàng*	照相
photographer	*shèyǐng shī*	摄影师
photography	*shèyǐng*	摄影
physics	*wùlǐ*	物理
piano	*gāngqín*	钢琴
pick (select)	*tiāo*	挑
pick up (get)	*qǔ*	取

DICTIONARY

pick up (meet)	jiē	接
pick up (retrieve from ground)	jiǎn	捡
pickled cabbage, hot	là báicài	辣白菜
pickled cucumber	suān huánggua	酸黄瓜
pickled mustard tuber, hot	zhàcài	榨菜
pickled vegetables	pàocài	泡菜
pictorial (magazine)	huàbào	画报
picture	túhuà	图画
picture book	huàcè	画册
piece (n)	kuài, jiàn, gè	块，件，个
pig	zhū	猪
pigeon	gēzi	鸽子
pill	yàowán	药丸
pillar	zhùzi	柱子
pillow	zhěntóu	枕头
pillowcase	zhěntóu tào	枕头套
pilose antler	lùróng	鹿茸
pilot (airplane)	fēixíngyuán	飞行员
pin (straight pin)	dàtóuzhēn	大头针
pine (tree)	sōng shù	松树
pineapple	bōluó	菠萝
ping-pong	pīngpāng qiú	乒乓球
Pingju Opera	píngjù	评剧
pink	fěnsè	粉色
pint	pǐntuō	品脱
place (n)	dìfang	地方
place of interest	kěkàn de dìfang	可看的地方
plains	píngyuán	平原
plan	jìhuà, dǎsuàn	计划，打算
plane	fēijī	飞机
plant (botanical)	zhíwù	植物
plaster (medicated)	gāoyào	膏药
plate (dish)	pánzi	盘子
plateau	gāoyuán	高原
platform	píngtái	平台
platform (train station)	yuètái	月台
play (a game)	wán	玩
play (sports: hit)	dǎ	打
play (sports: kick)	tī	踢

154

play (theater)	huàjù	话剧
player (in a game)	xuǎnshǒu	选手
player (sports team)	duìyuán	队员
playground	cāochǎng	操场
playwright	jùzuò jiā	剧作家
Please...	qǐng...	请……
pleased	hěn gāoxìng	很高兴
pliers	qiánzi	钳子
plot (story)	qíngjié	情节
plug (n)	chātóu	插头
plum	lǐzi	李子
plum blossom	méihuā	梅花
pneumonia	fèiyán	肺炎
poached egg	wòjīdàn, shuǐpūdàn	卧鸡蛋,水浦蛋
pocket	dōu, kǒudài	兜,口袋
pocket-size	xiùzhēn	袖珍
poet	shīrén	诗人
poetry	shī	诗
poker (game)	púkè	扑克
Polaroid camera	yícì chéngxiàng jī	一次成相机
Polaroid film	Pāilìdé xiàngzhǐ	拍立得相纸
police	jǐngchá	警察
police station	pàichūsuǒ	派出所
policy	zhèngcè	政策
polite	yǒu lǐmào	有礼貌
political bureau	zhèngzhìjú	政治局
politics	zhèngzhì	政治
polo	mǎqiú	马球
polyester (fiber)	qínglún	睛纶
pomegranate	shíliù	石榴
pomelo (grapefruit)	yòuzi	柚子
poor (not good)	bù hǎo	不好
poor (not rich)	qióng	穷
popular music	liúxíngqǔ	流行曲
porcelain	cíqì	瓷器
pork	zhūròu	猪肉
pork chop	zhūpái	猪排
porridge	zhōu	粥
port city	gǎngwān chéngshì	港湾城市
portable	biànxiéshì	便携式
porter	xínglǐ yuán	行李员
portrait	xiāoxiàng	肖像

DICTIONARY

portray	sùzào	塑造
possibility	kěnéng xìng	可能性
possible	kěnéng	可能
post (to mail)	jì	寄
post office	yóujú	邮局
postcard	míngxìnpiàn	明信片
poster	zhāotiēhuà	招贴画
pot (pan)	guō	锅
Potala Palace	Bùdálā gōng	布达拉宫
potato	tǔdòu	土豆
pottery	táoqì	陶器
pound (weight)	bàng	磅
pound sterling	yīngbàng	英磅
powder	fěnmò	粉末
power (authority)	quánlì	权力
power (energy)	néngyuán	能源
power (force)	lìliang	力量
practical (realistic)	shíjì	实际
practical (useful)	shíyòng	实用
practice (v)	liànxí	练习
prawn	dàxiā	大虾
pray	qídǎo	祈祷
prefer	gèng xǐhuan	更喜欢
pregnant	huáiyùn	怀孕
premier	zǒnglǐ	总理
prepare	zhǔnbèi	准备
prescription	yàofāng	药方
present (current)	mùqián	目前
president (corporate)	zǒngcái	总裁
president (national)	zǒngtǒng	总统
press (clothing)	tàng	烫
press (push down)	àn	按
pretty	piàoliang	漂亮
pride	zìháo, jiāo'ào	自豪,骄傲
principal (school)	xiàozhǎng	校长
print (art)	bǎnhuà	版画
print (photo)	xiàngpiàn	相片
print (v)	yìn	印
printed matter	yìnshuā pǐn	印刷品
private	sīrén	私人
probably	dàgài	大概
problem	wèntí	问题

process (n)	guòchéng	过程
producer	shēngchǎnzhě	生产者
product	chǎnpǐn	产品
production	shēngchǎn	生产
profession	zhíyè, hángyè	职业,行业
professor	jiàoshòu	教授
program (event)	jiémù	节目
program (theater handout)	jiémù dān	节目单
prohibited	jìnzhǐ	禁止
promise (n)	nuòyán	诺言
promise (v)	dāying	答应
prop (stage accessory)	dàojù	道具
province	shěng	省
provincial museum	shěng bówùguǎn	省博物馆
prune	lǐzi pǔ	李子脯
psychiatrist	jīngshénbìng yīshēng	精神病医生
psychologist	xīnlǐxuéjiā	心理学家
psychology	xīnlǐxué	心理学
psychosis	jīngshénbìng	精神病
pub	jiǔguǎn	酒馆
public	gōnggòng	公共
Public Security Bureau	gōng'ānjú	公安局
public bus	gōnggòng qìchē	公共汽车
public relations	gōnggòng guānxì	公共关系
public square	guǎngchǎng	广场
Puer tea	Pǔ'ěr chá	普洱茶
pull	lā	拉
pullover	tàotóu shān	套头衫
pulse	màibó	脉搏
punk	péngkè	朋客
puppet show	mù'ǒu xì	木偶戏
pure	chún	纯
purple	zǐsè	紫色
purpose	mùdì	目的
purse	qiánbāo	钱包
push	tuī	推
put	fàng	放
put away (in place)	fànghǎo	放好

DICTIONARY

Qin Emperor	Qínshǐhuáng	秦始皇
quail	ānchún	鹌鹑
quality	zhìliàng	质量
quantity	shùliàng	数量
quarantine	jiǎnyì	检疫
quart	kuātuō	夸脱
quarter (one-fourth)	sìfēn zhīyī	四分之一
quarter hour	kè, kèzhōng	刻，刻钟
quartet	sìchóngzòu	四重奏
question (n)	wèntí	问题
question (v)	tíwèn	提问
quick	kuài	快
quiet	ānjìng	安静
quilt	bèizi	被子
quinine	kuíníng	奎宁
quite	xiāngdāng	相当
quota	dìng'é	定额
rabbit	tùzi	兔子
racket (paddle)	qiúpāi	球拍
radiator	nuǎnqì	暖气
radio (broadcast)	guǎngbō	广播
radio (machine)	shōuyīnjī	收音机
radio program	guǎngbō jiémù	广播节目
radiologist	fàngshèkē yīshī	放射科医师
radish	xiǎo luóbo	小罗卜
railroad	tiělù	铁路
railway station	huǒchēzhàn	火车站
rain (n)	yǔ	雨
rain (v)	xiàyǔ	下雨
rain poncho	yǔpī	雨披
rainbow	cǎihóng	彩虹
raincoat	yǔyī	雨衣
raise (lift up)	tái qilai	抬起来
raisin	pútáo gān	葡萄干
ram	yáng, shānyáng	羊，山羊
ramie	zhùmá	苎麻
rape (vegetable)	yóucài	油菜
rash (on skin)	pízhěn	皮疹
rat	lǎoshǔ	老鼠
rate (price)	jiàgé	价格
rather (prefer to)	nìngyuàn	宁愿

ratio	bǐlì	比例
ravioli (boiled dumplings)	jiǎozi	饺子
rayon	rénzào sī	人造丝
razor	tìdāo	剃刀
razor blade	dāopiàn	刀片
read	dú, kàn	读，看
read aloud	niàn	念
read books	kàn shū	看书
real	zhēn	真
real estate agent	dìchǎn jīngjìrén	地产经纪人
really	zhēn	真的
reason (cause)	yuányīn	原因
reason (logic)	dàoli	道理
receipt (sales slip)	fāpiào	发票
receive (goods)	shōu	收
recently	jìnlái	近来
reception	jiēdài	接待
reception desk	jiēdài chù	接待处
reception personnel	jiēdài rényuán	接待人员
reception room	jiēdài shì	接待室
recipe (cooking)	shípǔ	食谱
recipient	shōujiàn rén, duìfāng	收件人，对方
recite	bèi	背
recommend	tūijiàn	推荐
record store	yīnxiǎng ménshìbù	音响门市部
recreation room	yùlè shì	娱乐室
red	hóng	红
red-crowned crane	dāndǐnghè	丹顶鹤
red paste (for seals)	yìnní	印泥
red wine	hóngjiǔ	红酒
reference (for study)	cānkǎo	参考
reform	gǎigé	改革
refreshment (cold drinks)	lěngyǐn	冷饮
refreshment (snacks)	xiǎochī	小吃
refreshment stand	xiǎochī tān	小吃摊
refrigerator	bīngxiāng	冰箱
refund	péicháng, péi	赔偿，赔
region	dìqū	地区
register	dēngjì	登记

DICTIONARY

registered (mail)	guàhào	挂号
registration desk	dēngjì chù	登记处
registration office (hospital)	guàhào chù	挂号处
regret	hòuhuǐ	后悔
regulation	guīdìng	规定
rehearsal	páiliàn	排练
relative (kin)	qīnqī	亲戚
relatives (kinfolk)	qīnshǔ	亲属
relevance	guānxi	关系
relief (sculpture)	fúdiāo	浮雕
remain (stay)	liú	留
remember	jìde	记得
Renault	Léinuò	雷诺
rent (v)	zū	租
rental fee	zūjīn	租金
repair	xiūlǐ	修理
repeat	chóngfù	重复
reprint (v)	jiāyìn	加印
reproduction (replica)	fùzhìpǐn	复制品
request	yāoqiú	要求
reroute	gǎihuàn	改换
research institute	yánjiūsuǒ	研究所
resemble	xiàng	象
reservations desk	yùdìng chù	预订处
reserve (v)	yùdìng	预订
reside	zhù	住
residence permit	jūliú zhèng	居留证
respect	zūnjìng	尊敬
rest (relax)	xiūxi	休息
restaurant	fànguǎn, cāntīng	饭馆，餐厅
result	jiēguǒ	结果
retail	língshòu	零售
retired worker	tuìxiū gōngrén	退休工人
return (come back)	huí	回
return (give back)	huán	还
return (merchandise)	tuì	退
reunion	tuánjù	团聚
review (critique)	pínglùn	评论
review (study again)	fùxí	复习
revolution	gémìng	革命

rheumatism	*fēngshī bìng*	风湿病
rib (n)	*lèigǔ*	肋骨
rice (cooked)	*mǐfàn*	米饭
rice (crop)	*dàozi*	稻子
rice congee	*xīfàn*	稀饭
rice paper	*xuānzhǐ*	宣纸
rich (prosperous)	*fù*	富
ride (a bicycle)	*qí*	骑
ride (a car)	*zuò*	坐
ride (an animal)	*qí*	骑
right (correct)	*duì*	对
right (direction)	*yòu*	右
right away	*mǎshàng*	马上
ring (jewelry)	*jièzhi*	戒指
riot	*bàoluàn*	暴乱
rise (go up, increase)	*shàngshēng*	上升
river	*hé, jiāng*	河，江
road	*lù, mǎlù*	路，马路
roadside	*lùbiān*	路边
roast (v)	*kǎo*	烤
roast pork bun	*chāshāo bāo*	叉烧包
roast suckling pig	*rǔzhū*	乳猪
rock-and-roll	*yáogǔn yuè*	摇滚乐
roll (n)	*juǎn*	卷
Rome	*Luómǎ*	罗马
roof	*fángdǐng*	房顶
room (in a building)	*fángjiān*	房间
room number	*fánghào*	房号
roommate	*tóngwū*	同屋
rooster	*gōngjī*	公鸡
rope skipping (Chinese)	*tiào píjīng*	跳皮筋
rosé (flower)	*méiguìhuā*	玫瑰花
rose, Chinese	*yuèjì*	月季
rough	*cūcāo*	粗糙
round (shape)	*yuán*	圆
round-trip ticket	*láihuí piào*	来回票
route	*lù*	路
row (column, line)	*pái*	排
rowboat	*huátǐng*	小船
rowing (sport)	*xiǎochuán*	划船
rubbing alcohol	*yīyòng jiǔjīng*	医用酒精

DICTIONARY

rude	cūbào	粗暴
rug	dìtǎn	地毯
ruins	yízhǐ	遗址
ruler (measuring stick)	chǐzi	尺子
runny nose	liú bíti	流鼻涕
rural	nóngcūn	农村
rush service	jiājí fúwù	加急服务
Russian (language)	Éyǔ	俄语
rusty	xiù le	锈了
sable	zǐdiāo	紫貂
Sacred Way	shéndào	神道
safety pin	biézhēn	别针
salad	shālā	沙拉
salary	gōngzī	工资
sales counter	shòuhuò tái, guìtái	售货台，柜台
sales manager	xiāoshòu jīnglǐ	销售经理
salesperson	tuīxiāoyuán	推销员
saline solution	shēnglǐ yánshuǐ	生理盐水
saliva	kǒushuǐ	口水
salt	yán	盐
salted duck egg	xián yādàn	咸鸭蛋
salty	xián	咸
same	yíyàng	一样
sample good	yàngpǐn	样品
San Francisco	Jiùjīnshān	旧金山
sand	shāzi	沙子
sandals	liángxié	凉鞋
sandalwood fan	tánxiāng shàn	檀香扇
sandwich	sānmingzhì	三明治
sanitary napkin	wèishēng jīn	卫生巾
Santana	Sāngtǎnà	桑塔纳
satellite	wèixīng	卫星
satisfied	mǎnyì	满意
satisfy	mǎnzú	满足
Saturday	xīngqī liù	星期六
sauce	jiàng	酱
sausage	xiāngcháng	香肠
sauteed	chǎo	炒
say	shuō	说
scallion	cōng	葱

scallop	gānbèi	干贝
scarf	wéijīn	围巾
scarlet fever	xīnghóngrè	猩红热
scenery	fēngjǐng	风景
schedule (timetable)	shíkè biǎo	时刻表
schizophrenia	jīngshén fēnliè zhèng	精神分裂症
school	xuéxiào	学校
school (of thought)	liúpài	流派
science	kēxué	科学
scientist	kēxuéjiā	科学家
scissors	jiǎndāo	剪刀
scrambled eggs	chǎo jīdàn	炒鸡蛋
screen (n)	píngfēng	屏风
screw (n)	luósīdīng	螺丝钉
screwdriver	luósīdāo	螺丝刀
script (play or film)	jiǎoběn	脚本
sculptor	diāosù jiā	雕塑家
sculpture	diāosù	雕塑
sea	hǎi	海
sea cucumber	hǎishēn	海参
seafood	hǎixiān	海鲜
season (n)	jìjié	季节
seat (n)	zuòwèi	座位
seat number	zuòhào	座号
seatbelt	ānquándài	安全带
second (fraction of time)	miǎo	秒
secret	mìmì	秘密
secretariat	shūjìchù	书记处
secretary, office	mìshū	秘书
security guard	ānquán rényuán	安全人员
see	kànjiàn	看见
see off	sòng	送
See you later	huítóujiàn	回头见
seems	hǎoxiàng	好象
self	zìjǐ, zìgě	自己，自个儿
self-portrait	zìhuàxiàng	自画像
self-timer (camera)	zìpāi	自拍
sell	mài	卖
seminar	yántǎohuì	研讨会
send a telegram	fā diànbào	发电报
send a telex	fā diànchuán	发电传

DICTIONARY

senior citizen	lǎoniánrén	老年人
sentence (n)	jùzi	句子
Seoul	Hànchéng	汉城
September	jiǔyuè	九月
serious (earnest)	rènzhēn	认真
serious (grave)	yánzhòng	严重
servant	púrén	仆人
service	fúwù	服务
service attendant	fúwùyuán	服务员
service desk	fúwùtái	服务台
service fee	fúwùfèi	服务费
service, religious	lǐbài	礼拜
sesame biscuit	shāobǐng	烧饼
sesame oil	máyóu	麻油
set (matching pieces)	tào	套
set (theater)	bùjǐng	布景
set design	bùjǐng shèjì	布景设计
settle the bill	jiézhàng	结帐
seven	qī	七
seventy	qīshí	七十
several	hǎo jǐge	好几个
sew	féng	缝
sex	xìng	性
shadow	yǐng	影
shadow puppet	píyǐng	皮影
shake hands	wòshǒu	握手
shampoo	xiāngbō	香波
Shanghai Opera	hùjù	沪剧
Shangri-La	Xiānggélǐlā	香格里拉
Shaoxing Opera	yuèjù, Shàoxīng xì	越剧, 绍兴戏
Shaoxing rice wine	Shàoxīng jiāfàn jiǔ	绍兴加饭酒
share (an expense)	fēntān	分摊
shark's fin soup	yúchì tāng	鱼翅汤
sharp (edge)	fēnglì	锋利
shattered	suì le	碎了
shave	guāliǎn	刮脸
shaver, electric	diàn tìdāo	电剃刀
she	tā	她
sheep	yáng	羊
sheet (of paper)	zhāng	张
sheets (linen)	chuángdān	床单
shelf	jiàzi	架子

shell mosaic	bèidiāohuà	贝雕画
Sheraton	Xǐláidēng	喜来登
shiny	shǎnguāng	闪光
ship (n)	chuán	船
ship (v)	hǎiyùn	海运
shipping company	hángyùn gōngsī	航运公司
shirt	chènshān	衬衫
shiver	fādǒu	发抖
shock (n)	xiūkè	休克
shoe	xié	鞋
shoe polish	xiéyóu	鞋油
shoehorn	xiébázi	鞋拔子
shoelaces	xiédài	鞋带
shooting (sport)	shèjī	射击
shop (n)	shāngdiàn, pùzi	商店,铺子
shopping	mǎi dōngxi	买东西
short (height)	ǎi	矮
short (length)	duǎn	短
should	yīnggāi	应该
shoulder (n)	jiānbǎng	肩膀
shoulder bag	bēibāo	背包
show (performance)	biǎoyǎn, yǎnchū	表演,演出
show (to demonstrate)	shìfàn	示范
shower	línyù	淋浴
shower cap	línyù mào	淋浴帽
shredded dried meat	ròusōng	肉松
shrimp	xiā	虾
shrine	jìtán	祭坛
shut	guān, bì	关,闭
shutter (camera)	kuàimén	快门
Siberia	Xībólìyà	西伯利亚
sickness	bìng	病
side (body)	cèlèi	侧肋
side (margin)	biān	边
sidewalk	rénxíngdào	人行道
sightsee	guānguāng, yóulǎn	观光,游览
sign (notice board)	páizi	牌子
sign (symbol)	biāojì	标记
signature	qiānmíng	签名
silent	wúshēng	无声
silk (pure)	zhēnsī	真丝

DICTIONARY

silk and brocade factory	*sīzhī chǎng*	丝织厂
silk cocoon factory	*sāosī chǎng*	缫丝厂
silk fabric	*sīchóu*	丝绸
silk mill	*sīchóu chǎng*	丝绸厂
silk products shop	*sīchóu shāngdiàn*	丝绸商店
Silk Road	*Sīchóu zhīlù*	丝绸之路
silkworm	*cán*	蚕
silver	*yín*	银
simulate	*mónī*	模拟
sing	*chànggē*	唱歌
Singapore	*Xīnjiāpō*	新加坡
singer	*gēchàng jiā*	歌唱家
single room	*dānjiān*	单间
sink	*shuǐchízi*	水池子
sister (older)	*jiějie*	姐姐
sister (younger)	*mèimei*	妹妹
sit	*zuò*	坐
six	*liù*	六
sixty	*liùshí*	六十
size (measurement)	*chǐcùn, guīgé*	尺寸,规格
size (number)	*hào*	号
sketch (art)	*sùxiě*	速写
sketch (design draft)	*cǎotú*	草图
skiing	*huáxuě*	滑雪
skill	*jìqiǎo*	技巧
skin	*pífū*	皮肤
skirt	*qúnzi*	裙子
sky	*tiānkōng*	天空
sky-diving	*tiàosǎn*	跳伞
sleep (v)	*shuìjiào*	睡觉
sleeping pill	*ānmián yào*	安眠药
slice (n)	*piàn*	片
slide (photo)	*huàndēng piàn*	幻灯片
slide film	*fǎnzhuǎn piàn*	反转片
slide mount	*huàndēngpiàn kuàng*	幻灯片框
slip (petticoat)	*chènqún*	衬裙
slippers	*tuōxié*	拖鞋
slow	*màn*	慢
small	*xiǎo*	小
smell (n)	*wèidao, wèi*	味道,味
smell (v)	*wén*	闻

smile	wēixiào	微笑
smoke cigarettes	chōuyān	抽烟
smoked fish	xūnyú	熏鱼
snack	xiǎochī, diǎnxin	小吃,点心
snake	shé	蛇
snow (n)	xuě	雪
snow (v)	xiàxuě	下雪
snow mountain	xuěshān	雪山
snow peas	xuědòu	雪豆
snuff bottle	bíyānhú	鼻烟壶
snuff box	bíyānhé	鼻烟盒
so (therefore)	suǒyǐ	所以
so-so	yìbān, mǎmǎhūhū	一般,马马虎虎
soap (n)	féizào	肥皂
soccer	zúqiú	足球
soccer match	zúqiú bǐsài	足球比赛
social dancing	jiāojì wǔ	交际舞
sociology	shèhuìxué	社会学
socket (electrical)	chāzuò	插座
socks	wàzi	袜子
soda pop	qìshuǐ	汽水
soda water	sūdá shuǐ	苏打水
sofa	shāfā	沙发
soft-seat	ruǎnxí	软席
soft-sleeper	ruǎnwò	软卧
softball	lěiqiú	垒球
soil (n)	tǔ, tǔrǎng	土,土壤
soldier	shìbīng, jūnrén	士兵,军人
solo (dance)	dúwǔ	独舞
solo (instrumental)	dúzòu	独奏
solo (vocal)	dúchàng	独唱
solution (method)	bànfǎ	办法
solve	jiějué	解决
some	yìxiē	一些
sometimes	yǒushí	有时
son	érzi	儿子
sonata	zòumíngqǔ	奏鸣曲
song	gēqǔ	歌曲
song-and-dance	gēwǔ	歌舞
song-and-dance troupe	gēwǔ tuán	歌舞团
Sony	Suǒní	索尼

DICTIONARY

soon	mǎshang, yīhuìr	马上，一会儿
sore (ache)	fāsuān, suān	发酸，酸
sore throat	hóulóng téng	喉咙疼
soreness	suānténg	酸疼
sorghum	gāoliáng	高梁
sound (n)	shēngyīn	声音
sound effect	yīnxiǎng	音响
soup	tāng	汤
soup noodles	tāngmiàn	汤面
sour	suān	酸
south	nán	南
South America	Nánměizhōu	南美洲
South China Sea	Nánhǎi	南海
Soviet Union	Sūlián	苏联
soy sauce	jiàngyóu	酱油
soybean	huángdòu	黄豆
soybean milk	dòujiāng	豆浆
space	kōngjiān	空间
space shuttle	hángtiān fēijī	航天飞机
spare time	yèyú shíjiān	业余时间
sparerib	páigǔ	排骨
speak	jiǎng	讲
special delivery (mail)	kuàidì	快递
speed limit	xiànsù	限速
spend	huā	花
spicy (hot)	là	辣
spinach	bōcài	菠菜
spine	jǐzhuī	脊椎
splinter (n)	cì	刺
spoke (wheel)	chētiáo	车条
spoon	sháozi	勺子
sporting goods	tǐyù yòngpǐn	体育用品
sports	yùndòng	运动
sports event	yùndòng xiàngmù	运动项目
spotlight	jùguāngdēng	聚光灯
spouse	pèi'ǒu	配偶
sprained	niǔshāng	扭伤
spring (season)	chūntiān	春天
spring roll	chūnjuǎn	春卷
square (area measure)	píngfāng	平方
square (shape)	fāng	方
square meter	píngfāng gōnglǐ	平方公里

squid	yóuyú	鱿鱼
stadium	tǐyùchǎng	体育场
stage (n)	wǔtái	舞台
stage (of progress)	jiēduàn	阶段
stainless steel	búxiùgāng	不锈钢
stairs	lóutī	楼梯
stale	bù xīnxiān	不新鲜
stamp (postage)	yóupiào	邮票
stamp collecting	jíyóu	集邮
stand (n)	jiàzi	架子
stand (v)	zhàn	站
standard	biāozhǔn	标准
standing committee	chángwù wěiyuánhuì	常务委员会
star (celebrity)	míngxīng	明星
star (n)	xīngxing	星星
state council	guówùyuàn	国务院
station (depot)	zhàn	站
station-to-station (phone)	jiàohào	叫号
stationery (writing paper)	xìnzhǐ	信纸
statue	sùxiàng, diāoxiàng	塑像，雕像
stay (live, spend time)	dāi	呆
steak (beef)	niúpái	牛排
steam (v)	zhēng	蒸
steamed bun	mántou	馒头
steamed dumpling	bāozi	包子
steamed twisted roll	huājuǎn	花卷
steel	gāng	钢
steep (in hot water)	pào	泡
steering wheel	fāngxiàngpán	方向盘
stele	shíbǎn, shízhù	石板，石柱
step (footstep)	bù	步
stereo system	zǔhé yīnxiǎng	组合音响
stew (v)	dùn	炖
stiff	jiāngyìng	僵硬
still (further)	hái	还
still (motionless)	bú dòng, tíngzhǐ	不动，停止
still (yet)	yīrán, réngrán	依然，仍然
still life painting	jìngwù huà	静物画
stir-fry	chǎo	抄
Stockholm	Sīdégē'ěrmó	斯德哥尔摩

stockings	chángtǒng wà	长筒袜
stocks (shares)	gǔpiào	股票
stomach	wèi, dùzi	胃, 肚子
stomachache	wèiténg	胃疼
stone (n)	shítou	石头
Stone Forest	Shílín	石林
stone rubbing	tàpiàn	拓片
stop (station)	zhàn	站
stop (v)	tíng	停
store (put away)	cúnfàng	存放
store (shop)	diàn, shāngdiàn	店, 商店
storyteller	shuōshū rén	说书人
storytelling	shuōshū	说书
straight	zhí	直
straits (waterway)	hǎixiá	海峡
strange	qíguài	奇怪
stranger (person)	mòshēng rén	陌生人
strawberry	cǎoméi	草莓
street	jiē	街
strength	lìliang, lìqi	力量, 力气
strict	yán	严
string (n)	shéngzi	绳子
string bean	sìjìdòu	四季豆
string instrument	xián yuèqì	弦乐器
string quartet	xiányuè sìchóngzòu	弦乐四重奏
striped	yǒu tiáowén de	有条纹的
stroke (paralysis)	zhòngfēng	中风
strong	qiángliè	强烈
struggle	dòuzhēng	斗争
stuck	dǔzhù le	堵住了
student	xuéshēng	学生
study (v)	xué	学
study abroad	liúxué	留学
stuffy (unventilated)	mēn	闷
stupid	bèn, chǔn	笨, 蠢
sturdy	jiēshi	结实
style	fēnggé	风格
suburb	jiāoqū	郊区
subway	dìtiě	地铁
subway station	dìtiě chēzhàn	地铁车站
success	chénggōng	成功
sugar	táng	糖

sugar cane	*gānzhe*	甘蔗
suit (clothing)	*xīzhuāng*	西装
suitcase	*xiāngzi*	箱子
suite (room)	*tàojiān*	套间
sulfa	*huáng'ān*	磺胺
summer	*xiàtiān*	夏天
Summer Palace	*Yíhéyuán*	颐和园
sun	*tàiyang*	太阳
Sun Yat-sen	*Sūn Zhōngshān*	孙中山
Sunday	*xīngqī rì*	星期日
sunlight	*yángguāng*	阳光
sunrise	*rìchū*	日出
sunset	*rìluò*	日落
sunstroke	*zhòngshǔ*	中暑
supervisor	*jiāndū rén*	监督人
support (an endeavor)	*zhīchí*	支持
surface mail	*píngxìn*	平信
surgeon	*wàikē yīshēng*	外科医生
surgery	*shǒushù*	手术
surgery department	*wàikē*	外科
surprised	*jīngya*	惊讶
sutra	*fójīng*	佛经
swallow (v)	*yàn*	咽
sweat (n)	*hàn*	汗
sweat (v)	*chūhàn*	出汗
sweater	*máoyī*	毛衣
sweatpants	*róngkù*	绒裤
sweatshirt	*róngyī*	绒衣
Sweden	*Ruìdiǎn*	瑞典
sweep	*sǎo*	扫
sweet	*tián*	甜
sweet-and-sour	*tángcù*	糖醋
sweet-and-sour pork	*gǔlǎo ròu*	古老肉
sweet potato	*báishǔ, shānyù*	白薯,山芋
swelling	*zhǒngzhùng*	肿胀
swim	*yóuyǒng*	游泳
swimming pool	*yóuyǒngchí*	游泳池
swimsuit	*yóuyǒngyī*	游泳衣
swing (playground)	*qiūqiān*	秋千
switchboard operator	*zǒngjī*	总机
Switzerland	*Ruìshì*	瑞士
sword bean	*dāodòu*	刀豆

DICTIONARY

Sydney	*Xīní*	悉尼
symbol	*biāozhì*	标志
symbolize	*xiàngzhēng*	象征
sympathetic	*tóngqíng*	同情·
symphony	*jiāoxiǎng yuè*	交响乐
symphony orchestra	*jiāoxiǎng yuèduì*	交响乐队
symptom	*zhèngzhuàng*	症状
synthetic (fiber)	*huàxiān*	化纤
syrup	*tángjiāng*	糖浆
system	*xìtǒng*	系统
T-intersection	*dīngzì lùkǒu*	丁字路口
T-shirt	*duǎnxiù shān*	短袖衫
table (n)	*zhuōzi*	桌子
tablecloth	*táibù, zhuōbù*	台布,桌布
tablespoon	*tóngsháo*	铜勺
tablet	*yàopiàn*	药片
taillight	*wěidēng*	尾灯
tailor (n)	*cáifeng*	裁缝
Taipei	*Táiběi*	台北
Taiwan	*Táiwān*	台湾
take (hold)	*ná*	拿
take (medication)	*fúyào*	服药
take a picture	*zhào zhāng xiàng*	照张相
take away	*názǒu*	拿走
take interest in	*duì...gǎn xìngqù*	对…感兴趣
take off (flights)	*qǐfēi*	起飞
talk (converse)	*tánhuà, jiāotán*	谈话,交谈
tamer	*xùnshòu yuán*	驯兽员
tampon	*wèishēng shuān*	卫生栓
Tang figurine (tri-colored)	*tángsāncǎi*	唐三彩
tangerine	*júzi*	橘子
tango	*tàngē*	探戈
Taoism	*dàojiào*	道教
tap (faucet)	*shuǐ lóngtóu*	水龙头
tape (cellophane)	*tòumíng jiāodài*	透明胶带
tape (sound)	*lùyīn cídài*	录音磁带
tape measure	*juǎnchǐ*	卷尺
tape recorder	*lùyīnjī*	录音机
tapestry	*bìtǎn*	壁毯
taro	*yùtou*	芋头

taste (n)	wèidao	味道
taste (v)	cháng	尝
tax (n)	shuì	税
taxi (n)	chūzū qìchē	出租汽车
tea	chá	茶
tea plantation (factory)	cháchǎng	茶场
tea set	chájù	茶具
tea shop	cháye diàn	茶叶店
teach	jiāo	教
teacher	lǎoshī, jiàoshī	老师，教师
teacup	chábēi	茶杯
teapot	cháhú	茶壶
teaspoon	xiǎo tóngsháo	小铜勺
technician	jìshùyuán	技术员
telegram	diànbào	电报
telephone (n)	diànhuà	电话
telephone (v)	dǎ diànhuà	打电话
telephone number	diànhuà hàomǎ	电话号码
television	diànshì	电视
television set	diànshìjī	电视机
television station	diànshì tái	电视台
telex	diànchuán	电传
telex call number	diànchuán guàhào	电传挂号
telex machine	diànchuánjī	电传机
tell	gàosù	告诉
temperature (general)	wēndù	温度
temperature (of body)	tǐwēn	体温
temple (Buddhist)	sì, miào	寺，庙
temple (Taoist)	guàn	观
Temple of Heaven	Tiāntán	天坛
ten	shí	十
ten thousand	wàn	万
tendon	jīn	筋
tennis	wǎngqiú	网球
terracotta figure	bīngmǎyǒng	兵马俑
terrible	kěpà, zāogāo	可怕，糟糕
test (exam)	kǎoshì	考试
tetanus	pò shāngfēng	破伤风
textile	fǎngzhī pǐn	纺织品
Thailand	Tàiguó	泰国
thank you	xièxie	谢谢

that	nà	那
that one	nàge, nèige	那个
theater	jùchǎng	剧场
theater troupe	jùtuán	剧团
their	tāmende	他们的
them	tāmen	他们
there	nàli, nàr	那里，那儿
therefore	yīncǐ	因此
thermal pants	miánmáo kù	棉毛裤
thermal shirt	miánmáo shān	棉毛衫
thermometer	wēndù biǎo	温度表
thermos	nuǎnshuǐpíng	暖水瓶
these	zhèxie	这些
they	tāmen	他们
thick (coarse)	cū	粗
thick (dense)	nóng	浓
thick (layer)	hòu	厚
thin (layer)	báo	薄
thin (slender)	shòu, xì	瘦，细
thin (sparse)	xī	稀
thing	dōngxi	东西
think (believe)	rènwéi	认为
thirsty	kě	渴
thirty	sānshí	三十
this	zhè	这
this one	zhège, zhèige	这个
this year	jīnnián	今年
those	nàxiē, nèixiē	那些
thousand	qiān	千
thousand-year egg	pídàn, sōnghuādàn	皮蛋，松花蛋
thread (n)	xiàn	线
three	sān	三
Three Gorges	Sānxiá	三峡
three delicacies soup	sānxiān tāng	三鲜汤
three-dimensional	lìtǐ	立体
three-prong plug	sānxiàng chātóu	三相插头
throat	hóulóng	喉咙
throw	rēng	扔
throw away	rēng diào	扔掉
thunder	léi	雷
Thursday	xīngqī sì	星期四
Tibet	Xīzàng	西藏

ticket	*piào*	票
ticket office	*shòupiào chù*	售票处
ticket seller	*shòupiàoyuán*	售票员
tie (necktie)	*lǐngdài*	领带
tie up	*kǔn qilai*	捆起来
tiger	*lǎohǔ*	老虎
tiger balm	*qīngliángyóu*	清凉油
tight	*jǐn*	紧
tile (n)	*wǎ*	瓦
timber	*mùliào*	木料
time (n)	*shíjiān*	时间
time (occasion)	*cì*	次
time period (historic)	*niándài*	年代
timer	*jìshí qì*	计时器
timetable	*shíkè biǎo*	时刻表
tip (gratuity)	*xiǎofèi*	小费
tire (wheel)	*chētāi*	车胎
tired	*lèi*	累
toast (bread)	*kǎo miànbāo*	烤面包
today	*jīntiān*	今天
toe	*jiǎozhǐ*	脚趾
toilet	*cèsuǒ*	厕所
toilet paper	*wèishēng zhǐ*	卫生纸
Tokyo	*Dōngjīng*	东京
tomato	*xīhóngshì, fānqié*	西红柿, 番茄
tomato sauce	*fānqié jiàng*	番茄酱
tomb	*fénmù*	坟墓
tombs, imperial	*líng*	陵
tomorrow	*míngtiān*	明天
ton	*dūn*	吨
tongue	*shétou*	舌头
tonight	*jīnwǎn*	今晚
too (also)	*yě*	也
too (excessive)	*tài*	太
tool	*gōngjù*	工具
tooth	*yá*	牙
toothache	*yáténg*	牙疼
toothbrush	*yáshuā*	牙刷
toothpaste	*yágāo*	牙膏
toothpick	*yáqiān*	牙签
top (height)	*dǐng*	顶

DICTIONARY

torn	*pòle*	破了
Toronto	*Duōlúnduō*	多伦多
tortoise	*wūguī*	乌龟
touch-me-not	*fèngxiānhuā*	凤仙花
tour escort	*lǐngduì*	领队
tour group	*lǚyóu tuán*	旅游团
tourist	*lǚkè*	旅客
tournament	*bǐsài*	比赛
toward	*wǎng, xiàng*	往，向
towel	*máojīn*	毛巾
town	*zhèn*	镇
township	*xiāng*	乡
toy	*wánjù*	玩具
toy store	*wánjù diàn*	玩具店
Toyota	*Fēngtián*	丰田
track and field	*tiánjìng*	田径
tractor	*tuōlājī*	拖拉机
trade (business)	*màoyì*	贸易
traditional	*chuántǒng*	传统
traffic	*jiāotōng*	交通
traffic circle	*jiāotōng huándǎo*	交通环岛
traffic jam	*dǔchē*	堵车
traffic light	*hónglǜdēng*	红绿灯
tragedy	*bēijù*	悲剧
train (railroad)	*huǒchē*	火车
train station	*huǒchē zhàn*	火车站
training	*xùnliàn*	训练
tranquilizer	*zhènjìngjì*	镇静剂
transfer (bus, train)	*dǎo, huàn*	倒，换
transformer (voltage)	*biànyāqì*	变压器
transit visa	*guòjìng qiānzhèng*	过境签证
translate	*fānyì*	翻译
translator	*fānyì*	翻译
transparent	*tòuming*	透明
travel	*lǚxíng*	旅行
travel permit	*lǚyóu xǔkězhèng*	旅游许可证
travel service (agency)	*lǚxíngshè*	旅行社
traveler's check	*lǚxíng zhīpiào*	旅行支票
traveling bag	*lǚxíng bāo*	旅行包
tree	*shù*	树
tribe	*bùluò, jiāzú*	部落，家族

trick (v)	*piàn*	骗
tricycle (child's)	*értóng chē*	儿童车
tricycle (pedicab)	*sānlún chē*	三轮车
trim	*xiūjiǎn*	修剪
trio (instrumental)	*sānchóngzòu*	三重奏
trip (travel)	*lǚxíng*	旅行
tripod	*sānjiǎojià*	三角架
trolley	*wúguǐ diànchē*	无轨电车
truck (n)	*kǎchē*	卡车
true	*zhēn*	真
trunk (car)	*xíngli xiāng*	行李箱
trunk (luggage)	*píxiāng*	皮箱
truth	*zhēnlǐ*	真理
try	*shì yíxia*	试一下
tuberculosis	*fèi jiéhé*	肺结核
Tuesday	*xīngqī èr*	星期二
tug of war	*báhé*	拔河
turn (a corner)	*guǎiwān*	拐湾
turn around (head back)	*diàotóu, huízhuǎn*	调头，回转
turn off (to shut off)	*guān*	关
turn on (to switch on)	*kāi*	开
turnip	*luóbo*	萝卜
turtle	*wūguī*	乌龟
twenty	*èrshí*	二十
twin bed	*dānrén chuáng*	单人床
twin room	*shuāngrén fángjiān*	双人房间
two (the number)	*èr*	二
two (the quantity)	*liǎng*	两
two-prong plug (flat prongs)	*píngjiǎo chātóu*	平角插头
two-prong plug (round prongs)	*yuánjiǎo chātóu*	圆角插头
type (kind)	*zhǒnglèi*	种类
typewriter	*dǎzìjī*	打字机
typhoid	*shānghán*	伤寒
typhoon	*táifēng*	台风
typhus	*bānzhěn shānghán*	斑疹伤寒
typist	*dǎzìyuán*	打字员

DICTIONARY

ugly	chǒu, nánkàn	丑，难看
ulcer	kuìyáng	溃疡
umbrella	yǔsǎn	雨伞
uncle	shūshu	叔叔
(see Appendix H)		
under	zài...xiàmiàn	在…下面
underground (adj)	dìxià	地下
underpass	dìxià tōngdào	地下通道
understand	dǒng	懂
underwear	nèiyī	内衣
uniform	zhìfú	制服
unit (organization)	dānwèi	单位
united	liánhé	联合
United Nations	Liánhéguó	联合国
United States	Měiguó	美国
university	dàxué	大学
until	dào...wéizhǐ	到…为止
up	shàng	上
upstairs	lóushàng	楼上
urban	chéngshì	城市
urinate	xiǎobiàn	小便
US dollar	měiyuán	美元
use (n)	zuòyòng	作用
use (v)	yòng	用
useful	yǒu yòng	有用
usually	tōngcháng, jīngcháng	通常，经常
vacation (n)	jiàqī, jià	假期，假
vacation, spend a	dùjià	度假
vaccination certificate	fángyì zhèng	防疫证
vacuum cleaner	xīchén qì	吸尘器
vague	mōhu	模糊
valley	shāngǔ	山谷
valuable object	guìzhòng wùpǐn	贵重物品
value (n)	jiàzhí	价值
van (mini-bus)	miànbāochē	面包车
Vancouver	Wēngēhuá	温哥华
vase	huāpín	花瓶
vegetable	shūcài	蔬菜
vegetarian food	sùshí	素食
ventilation	tōngfēng	通风

vermicelli (dried)	*guàmiàn*	挂面
vertical flute (bamboo)	*xiāo*	箫
very	*hěn*	很
vest	*bèixīn*	背心
vice-president (national)	*fù zǒngtǒng*	副总统
video camera	*shèxiàng jī*	摄像机
video cassette recorder	*lùxiàng jī*	录像机
videotape	*lùxiàng cídài*	录像磁带
Vietnam	*Yuènán*	越南
view (scenery)	*jǐngsè*	景色
viewfinder	*qǔjǐngqì*	取景器
village	*cūnzhuāng*	村庄
village fair	*jíshì*	集市
villain	*ègùn*	恶棍
vinegar	*cù*	醋
violin	*xiǎotíqín*	小提琴
visa	*qiānzhèng*	签证
visa office (PSB)	*gōng'ānjú wàiguǎnchù*	公安局外管处
visit	*cānguān, fǎngwèn*	参观,访问
visit relatives	*tànqīn*	探亲
vocabulary	*cíhuì liàng*	词汇量
vodka	*fútèjiā*	伏特加
voice (n)	*sǎngzi*	嗓子
volleyball	*páiqiú*	排球
voltage	*diànyā*	电压
voltage converter	*biànyāqì*	变压器
volts, 110	*yìbǎi yīshí fú*	100 伏
volts, 220	*èrbǎi èrshí fú*	220 伏
volume (book)	*juàn*	卷
volume (sound)	*yīnliàng*	音量
vomit	*ǒutù*	呕吐
wage (salary)	*gōngzī*	工资
waist	*yāo*	腰
waist drum	*yāogǔ*	腰鼓
wait	*děng*	等
waiter or waitress	*fúwùyuán*	服务员
waiting lounge	*hòukè shì*	候客室
wake up (self)	*xǐnglái*	醒来

DICTIONARY

wake up (someone else)	jiàoxǐng	叫醒
walk	zǒu, sànbù	走，散步
Walkman (personal stereo)	dānfàng jī	单放机
wall	qiáng	墙
wallet	píjiāzi	皮夹子
walnut	hétao	核桃
waltz (dance)	huá'ěrzī	华尔兹
waltz (music)	yuánwǔqǔ	圆舞曲
want (v)	yào	要
war	zhànzhēng	战争
warm (adj)	nuǎnhe	暖和
warm (personality)	rèqíng	热情
wash (v)	xǐ	洗
washcloth	xǐliǎn jīn	洗脸巾
Washington DC	Huáshèngdùn Tèqū	华盛顿特区
waste (v)	làngfèi	浪费
wastebasket	zhǐlǒu	纸篓
watch (v)	kàn	看
watch (wristwatch)	shǒubiǎo	手表
watchband	biǎodài	表带
water (n)	shuǐ	水
water caltrop	língjiǎo	菱角
water chestnut	bíqì	荸荠
water lily	shuǐfúlián	水浮莲
water polo	shuǐqiú	水球
water-skiing	huáshuǐ yùndòng	划水运动
watercolors	shuǐcǎi	水彩
waterfall	pùbù	瀑布
watermelon	xīguā	西瓜
wavy	bōlàngshì	波浪式
way (direction)	fāngxiàng	方向
way (method)	fāngfǎ	方法
we	wǒmen	我们
weak	ruò	弱
wealth	cáifù	财富
wealth (symbol)	lù	禄
wear	chuān, dài	穿，戴
weasel	huángshǔláng	黄鼠狼
weather	tiānqì	天气
weather forecast	tiānqì yùbào	天气预报

weave	*biānzhī*	编织
weaving (n)	*zhīpǐn*	织品
wedding	*hūnlǐ*	婚礼
Wednesday	*xīngqī sān*	星期三
week	*xīngqī*	星期
weekend	*zhōumò*	周末
weekly (magazine)	*zhōubào*	周报
weight-lifting	*jǔzhòng*	举重
welcome	*huānyíng*	欢迎
well (adv)	*hǎo*	好
well (n)	*jǐng*	井
west	*xī*	西
West Germany	*Xīdé*	西德
West Lake	*Xīhú*	西湖
Western meal	*xīcān*	西餐
Western menu	*xīcān càipǔ*	西餐菜谱
Western toilet	*zuòshì cèsuǒ*	坐式厕所
wet (adj)	*shī*	湿
what	*shénme*	什么
wheat	*màizi*	麦子
wheel	*lúnzi*	轮子
wheelchair	*lúnyǐ*	轮椅
when	*shénme shíhòu*	什么时候
where	*nǎlǐ, nǎr*	哪里，哪儿
which	*nǎge, nèige*	哪个
whiskey	*wēishìjì*	威士忌
white	*bái*	白
White Peony tea	*Shòuméi chá*	寿眉茶
white edible fungus	*yín'ěr*	银耳
white liquor, Chinese	*báijiǔ*	白酒
white wine	*bái pútao jiǔ*	白葡萄酒
who (question)	*shéi*	谁
whole	*zhěnggè*	整个
wholesale	*pīfā*	批发
why	*wèi shénme*	为什么
wide	*kuān*	宽
width	*kuāndù*	宽度
wife	*qīzi, fūrén, àirén*	妻子，夫人，爱人
wildlife preserve	*zìrán bǎohù qū*	自然保护区
will (determination)	*yìzhì*	意志
will (future tense)	*yào*	要
willow tree	*liǔshù*	柳树

DICTIONARY

win	yíng	赢
wind (n)	fēng	风
wind instrument (music)	guǎn yuèqì	管乐器
window	chuānghu	窗户
windshield	dǎngfēng bōlí	挡风玻璃
windsurfing	fānbǎn yùndòng	帆板运动
windy	yǒufēng	有风
wine	pútáo jiǔ	葡萄酒
wine glass	jiǔbēi	酒杯
winter	dōngtiān	冬天
winter melon	dōngguā	冬瓜
wipe	cā	擦
wish (n)	yuànwàng	愿望
wishing you...	zhù nǐ...	祝你……
within	zài...yǐnèi	在…以内
wok	chǎocài guō	炒菜锅
woman	fùnǚ	妇女
women's bike	nǚchē	女车
wonderful	fēicháng jīngcǎi	非常精彩
wonton	húndùn	馄饨
wood	mùtou	木头
woodcut	mùbǎn huà	木版画
wool	yángmáo	羊毛
word	zì	字
work (art, literature)	zuòpǐn	作品
work (job)	gōngzuò	工作
work quota	gōngzuò liàng	工作量
work unit	dānwèi	单位
worker	gōngrén	工人
worker's cap	yāshémào	鸭舌帽
workshop	chējiān	车间
world	shìjiè	世界
World War II	èr cì dàzhàn	二次大战
worry	dānxīn	担心
worse	gènghuài, gèngzāo	更坏，更糟
would like to	xiǎng	想
wound (n)	shāngkǒu	伤口
wrap	bāo	包
wrapping paper	bāozhuāng zhǐ	包装纸
wrench (hardware)	bānshou	搬手
wrestling	shuāijiāo	摔跤

wrist	shǒuwàn	手腕
write	xiě	写
write down	xiě xià	写下
writer	zuòjiā	作家
writing brush,	máobǐ	毛笔
wrong	cuò le, bú duì	错了,不对
X-ray	X-guāng	X 光
Xerox	fùyìn	复印
(see duplication)		
		牦牛
yak	máoniú	长江
Yangtze River	Chángjiāng	码
yard (3 feet)	mǎ	年
year	nián	岁
years old (age)	suì	黄
yellow	huáng	黄花鱼
yellow croaker	huánghuāyú	黄河
Yellow River	Huánghé	黄海
Yellow Sea	Huánghǎi	日元
yen	Rìyuán	昨天
yesterday	zuótiān	还
yet	hái	酸奶
yogurt	suānnǎi	你
you	nǐ	你们
you (plural)	nǐmen	您
you (polite form)	nín	年青,小
young	niánqīng, xiǎo	小伙子
young man	xiǎo huǒzi	青年
young people	qīngnian	年青女人
young woman	niánqīng nǚren	你的
your	nǐde	你们的
your (plural)	nǐmende	蒙古包
yurt	měnggǔbāo	
		斑马线
zebra crosswalk	bānmǎ xiàn	零
zero	líng	拉链
zipper	lāliàn	瑟
zither, 25-string	sè	古琴
zither, 7-string	gǔqín	筝
zither, many-stringed	zhēng	动物园
zoo	dòngwùyuán	

Chinese-English Supplement

This supplement provides English definitions of Chinese terms which are likely to be mentioned to the traveler. In particular, attention has been given to medical vocabulary, names of Chinese foods and products, and words which the traveler might hear in reply to the question *Zhèige shì shénme?* (What is this?)

阿斯匹林	*āsīpǐlín*	aspirin
阿姨	*āyí*	auntie
艾滋病	*àizībìng*	AIDS
鹌鹑	*ānchún*	quail
安眠药	*ānmián yào*	sleeping pill
按摩	*ànmó*	massage
八宝饭	*bābǎofàn*	eight precious rice
拔丝苹果	*básī píngguǒ*	honey crystalized apples
拔牙	*báyá*	extract a tooth
白菜	*báicài*	bok choy; cabbage
白果	*báiguǒ*	ginkgo
白酒	*báijiǔ*	Chinese white liquor
白杨树	*báiyángshù*	aspen tree
百	*bǎi*	hundred
百货商店	*bǎihuò shāngdiàn*	department store
柏树	*bǎishù*	cypress tree
斑疹伤寒	*bānzhěn shānghán*	typhus
版画	*bǎnhuà*	print
包车	*bāochē*	hired car
包子	*bāozi*	steamed dumpling
鲍鱼	*bàoyú*	abalone
悲剧	*bēijù*	tragedy
荸荠	*bíqì*	water chestnut
鼻通	*bítōng*	decongestant
鼻子	*bízi*	nose
闭路电视	*bìlù diànshì*	cable TV
避孕用品	*bìyùn yòng pǐn*	contraceptives
便秘	*biàn bì*	constipation
宾馆	*bīnguǎn*	guesthouse, hotel

SUPPLEMENT

冰球	**bīngqiú**	ice hockey
冰糖葫芦	**bīngtáng húlu**	candied haws
丙纶	**bǐnglún**	acrylic
菠菜	**bōcài**	spinach
菠萝	**bōluó**	pineapple
不锈钢	**búxiùgāng**	stainless steel
补牙	**bǔyá**	fill a tooth
菜豆	**càidòu**	kidney bean
菜花	**càihuā**	cauliflower
菜心	**càixīn**	cabbage heart
餐厅	**cāntīng**	dining room, restaurant
蚕	**cán**	silkworm
蚕豆	**cándòu**	broad bean
草药	**cǎoyào**	herbal medicine
侧肋	**cèlèi**	side
厕所	**cèsuǒ**	toilet
叉烧包	**chāshāo bāo**	roast pork bun
茶花	**cháhuā**	camelia
产科病房	**chǎnkē bìngfáng**	maternity ward
长寿	**chángshòu**	longevity
肠子	**chángzi**	bowels
车间	**chējiān**	workshop
城门	**chéngmén**	city gate
城墙	**chéngqiáng**	city wall
成语	**chéngyǔ**	idiom
抽筋	**chōujīn**	cramp
出口货	**chūkǒu huò**	export goods
出血	**chūxuè**	hemorrhage
传染	**chuánrǎn**	infection
船闸	**chuánzhá**	ship lock
春节	**chūnjié**	Chinese New Year
春卷	**chūnjuǎn**	spring roll
葱	**cōng**	scallion
葱头	**cōngtóu**	onion
醋	**cù**	vinegar
催吐剂	**cuītùjì**	emetic
大白菜	**dà báicài**	Chinese cabbage
大便	**dàbiàn**	bowel movement
大理石	**dàlǐshí**	marble
大麦	**dàmài**	barley

大虾	*dàxiā*	prawn
丹顶鹤	*dāndǐnghè*	red-crowned crane
单位	*dānwèi*	work unit; organization
单行线	*dānxíng xiàn*	one-way street
单元	*dānyuán*	housing unit; doorway
蛋花汤	*dànhuātāng*	egg-drop soup
刀豆	*dāodòu*	sword bean
登机牌	*dēngjīpái*	boarding pass
登记处	*dēngjì chù*	registration desk
低	*dī*	low
笛子	*dízi*	bamboo flute
地铁	*dìtiě*	subway
点穴法	*diǎnxuèfǎ*	acupressure
电报	*diànbào*	telegram
电报挂号	*diànbào guàhào*	cable address
电传	*diànchuán*	telex
电传挂号	*diànchuán guàhào*	telex call number
电疗	*diànliáo*	electrotherapy
貂	*diāo*	marten
丁香	*dīngxiāng*	lilac
丁香酒	*dīngxiāng jiǔ*	clove wine
丁字路口	*dīngzì lùkǒu*	T-intersection
定额	*dìng'é*	quota
冬菇	*dōnggū*	black mushroom
冬瓜	*dōngguā*	winter melon
豆瓣酱	*dòubàn jiàng*	hot bean sauce
豆腐	*dòufu*	beancurd
豆腐干	*dòufu gān*	dried beancurd
豆浆	*dòujiāng*	soybean milk
豆沙	*dòushā*	sweetened bean paste
豆芽	*dòuyá*	bean sprout
豆子	*dòuzi*	bean
杜鹃花	*dùjuānhuā*	azalea
对	*duì*	correct
对不起	*duìbuqǐ*	excuse me, sorry
恶心	*ěxīn*	nauseous
儿科	*érkē*	pediatrics department
耳鼻喉科	*ěr-bí-hóu kē*	ear-nose-throat department
二胡	*èrhú*	2-string fiddle

SUPPLEMENT

发抖	*fādǒu*	shiver
发炎	*fāyán*	inflammation, infection
蕃茄	*fānqié*	tomato
饭	*fàn*	rice
饭店	*fàndiàn*	hotel; restaurant
饭馆	*fànguǎn*	restaurant
饭后	*fànhòu*	after meals
饭前	*fànqián*	before meals
防疫证	*fángyì zhèng*	vaccination certificate
放射科	*fàngshèkē*	radiology department
翡翠	*fěicuì*	chrysolite
肺	*fèi*	lung
肺结核	*fèi jiéhé*	tuberculosis
肺炎	*fèiyán*	pneumonia
坟墓	*fénmù*	tomb
风湿病	*fēngshī bìng*	rheumatism
凤仙花	*fèngxiānhuā*	touch-me-not
佛经	*fójīng*	sutra
福	*fú*	symbol for luck
服务费	*fúwùfèi*	service fee
服务员	*fúwùyuán*	service attendant
服装店	*fúzhuāng diàn*	clothing store
妇科	*fùkē*	gynecology department
付食品	*fùshí pǐn*	nonstaple food
腹泻	*fùxiè*	diarrhea
复制品	*fùzhìpǐn*	reproduction
芥菜	*gàicài*	leaf mustard
芥蓝	*gàilán*	Chinese broccoli
肝	*gān*	liver
干咸鱼	*gān xián yú*	dried minced fish
干杯!	*Gānbēi!*	Cheers!
干贝	*gānbèi*	scallop
肝炎	*gānyán*	hepatitis
柑子	*gānzi*	mandarin orange
橄榄	*gǎnlǎn*	olive
高	*gāo*	high
高尔夫	*gāo'ěrfū*	golf
高粱	*gāoliáng*	sorghum
膏药	*gāoyào*	medicated plaster
高原	*gāoyuán*	highland
鸽子	*gēzi*	pigeon
隔离病房	*gélí bìngfáng*	isolation ward

蛤蜊	gěli	clams
公安局	gōng'ānjú	Public Security Bureau
公斤	gōngjīn	kilogram
公里	gōnglǐ	kilometer
公路	gōnglù	highway
公顷	gōngqīng	hectare
工艺美术	gōngyì měishù	arts and crafts
公寓	gōngyù	apartment
工资	gōngzī	slary
工作量	gōngzuò liàng	work quota
鼓楼	gǔlóu	drum tower
古琴	gǔqín	7-string zither
骨头	gǔtou	bone
挂面	guàmiàn	vermicelli
观察室	guānchá shì	observation ward
关节	guānjié	joints
关节炎	guānjié yán	arthritis
关系	guānxi	connection, relation
规定	guīdìng	regulation
桂花	guìhuā	cassia
桂花酒	guìhuā jiǔ	cassia wine
锅贴	guōtiē	fried dumplings
国画	guóhuà	traditional Chinese painting
国务院	guówùyuàn	state council
过敏症	guòmǐn zhèng	allergy
哈密瓜	hāmìguā	Hami melon
海关申报单	hǎiguān shēnbào dān	customs declaration
海狸	hǎilí	beaver
海米	hǎimǐ	dried shrimps
海参	hǎishēn	sea cucumber
海棠	hǎitáng	Chinese crabapple
海鲜	hǎixiān	seafood
海蜇	hǎizhé	jellyfish
含片	hánpiàn	throat lozenges
汗	hàn	sweat
蚝	háo	oyster
蚝油	háoyóu	oyster sauce
好莱坞	Hǎoláiwū	Hollywood
荷花	héhuā	lotus
核桃	hétao	walnut

SUPPLEMENT

鹤	*hè*	crane
红茶	*hóngchá*	black tea
红绿灯	*hónglǜdēng*	traffic light
红烧	*hóngshāo*	braised in brown sauce
红薯	*hóngshǔ*	sweet potato
喉咙	*hóulóng*	throat
忽必烈	*Hūbiliè*	Kublai Khan
沪剧	*hùjù*	Shanghai Opera
护照	*hùzhào*	passport
花菜	*huācài*	cauliflower
花粉热	*huāfěn rè*	hay fever
花卷	*huājuǎn*	steamed twisted roll
花生	*huāshēng*	peanut
华侨	*Huáqiáo*	overseas Chinese
化疗	*huàliáo*	chemotherapy
化纤	*huàxiān*	synthetic
槐树	*huáishù*	locust tree
怀孕	*huáiyùn*	pregnant
磺胺	*huáng'ān*	sulfa
黄豆	*huángdòu*	soybean
黄瓜	*huángguā*	cucumber
黄花鱼	*huánghuāyú*	yellow croaker
黄鼠狼	*huángshǔláng*	weasel
昏迷	*hūnmí*	coma
馄饨	*húndùn*	wonton
火锅	*huǒguō*	hot pot
火腿	*huǒtuǐ*	ham
霍乱	*huòluàn*	cholera
机场费	*jīchǎng fèi*	airport departure tax
鸡冠花	*jīguānhuā*	cock's comb
肌肉	*jīròu*	muscle
急救站	*jíjiù zhàn*	first-aid station
集市	*jíshì*	village fair
集邮	*jíyóu*	stamp collecting
急诊室	*jízhěn shì*	emergency room
脊椎	*jǐzhuī*	spine
家乡	*jiāxiāng*	native place
夹竹桃	*jiāzhútáo*	oleander
驾驶执照	*jiàshǐ zhízhào*	driver's license
煎饼	*jiānbǐng*	crepe, egg pancake
减价	*jiǎnjià*	price reduction

简谱	*jiǎnpǔ*	numbered music notation
检疫	*jiǎnyì*	quarantine
健康表	*jiànkāng biǎo*	health declaration
健美操	*jiànměi cāo*	aerobics
江豆	*jiāngdòu*	green long bean
奖金	*jiǎngjīn*	bonus
酱油	*jiàngyóu*	soy sauce
饺子	*jiǎozi*	boiled dumplings, ravioli
节目	*jiémù*	program; event
结帐	*jiézhàng*	settle the bill
借光	*jièguāng*	excuse me, make way
芥末	*jièmo*	mustard
筋	*jīn*	tendon
金桔	*jīnjú*	kumquat
金丝猴	*jīnsīhóu*	golden-haired monkey
金鱼	*jīnyú*	goldfish
金针	*jīnzhēn*	day-lily bud
进口货	*jìnkǒu huò*	import goods
京胡	*jīnghú*	Beijing opera fiddle
经济日报	*Jīngjì Rìbào*	Economic Daily
京剧	*jīngjù*	Beijing Opera
痉挛	*jīngluán*	convulsion
精神病	*jīngshénbìng*	psychosis
精神分裂	*jīngshén fēnliè*	schizophrenia
静脉注射	*jìngmài zhùshè*	intravenous injection
酒	*jiǔ*	alcoholic beverage
韭菜	*jiǔcài*	Chinese chives
酒精	*jiǔjīng*	alcohol
居留证	*jūliú zhèng*	residence permit
局部麻醉	*júbù mázuì*	local anesthesia
菊花	*júhuā*	chrysanthemum
剧场	*jùchǎng*	theater
开水	*kāishuǐ*	boiled water
凯乐	*Kǎiyuè*	Hyatt
抗生素	*kàngshēngsù*	antibiotic
咳嗽	*késòu*	cough
口水	*kǒushuǐ*	saliva
苦瓜	*kǔguā*	bitter gourd
奎宁	*kuíníng*	quinine

SUPPLEMENT

溃疡	*kuìyáng*	ulcer
昆曲	*kūnqǔ*	Kunshan Opera
拉肚子	*lā dùzi*	diarrhea
辣酱	*làjiàng*	hot sauce
辣椒	*làjiāo*	chilli pepper
腊梅	*làméi*	allspice
腊肉	*làròu*	dried minced meat
兰花	*lánhuā*	orchid
篮球	*lánqiú*	basketball
劳驾	*láojia*	excuse me, make way
老家	*lǎojiā*	ancestral place
肋骨	*lèigǔ*	rib
梨	*lí*	pear
理发店	*lǐfà diàn*	barbershop
李子	*lǐzi*	plum
痢疾	*lìji*	dysentery
荔枝	*lìzhī*	lychee
栗子	*lìzi*	chestnut
莲花	*liánhuā*	lotus
莲子	*liánzǐ*	lotus seed
粮票	*liángpiào*	grain coupon
烈士	*lièshì*	martyr
菱角	*língjiǎo*	water caltrop
零钱	*língqián*	coins, small bills
零售	*língshòu*	retail
流感	*liúgǎn*	flu
柳树	*liǔshù*	willow tree
龙井茶	*Lóngjǐng chá*	Dragon Well tea
龙虾	*lóngxiā*	lobster
龙眼	*lóngyǎn*	longan fruit
禄	*lù*	symbol for wealth
鹿	*lù*	deer
路口	*lùkǒu*	intersection, crossroad
鹿茸	*lùróng*	pilose antler
旅馆	*lǚguǎn*	hotel
旅社	*lǚshè*	hostel
旅行社	*lǚxíngshè*	travel service
绿茶	*lǜchá*	green tea
绿豆	*lǜdòu*	mung bean
萝卜	*luóbo*	turnip
麻花	*máhuā*	fried sesame twists

麻将	*májiàng*	mah-jongg
麻油	*máyóu*	sesame oil
麻疹	*mázhěn*	measles
麻醉	*mázuì*	anesthesia
吗啡	*mǎfēi*	morphine
马可·波罗	*Mǎkě Bōluó*	Marco Polo
玛瑙	*mǎnǎo*	agate
脉膊	*màibó*	pulse
麦子	*màizi*	wheat
馒头	*mántou*	steamed bread
慢车	*mànchē*	local bus or train
慢性	*mànxìng*	chronic
芒果	*mángguǒ*	mango
牦牛	*máoniú*	yak
茅台	*máotái*	Maotai liquor
玫瑰花	*méiguīhuā*	rose
梅花	*méihuā*	plum blossom
米	*mǐ*	meter
米老鼠	*Mǐlǎoshǔ*	Mickey Mouse
棉	*mián*	cotton
免费	*miǎnfèi*	free of charge
面条	*miàntiáo*	noodles
蘑菇	*mógu*	mushroom
墨	*mò*	ink stick
末班车	*mò bān chē*	last bus or train
墨斗鱼	*mòdǒuyú*	cuttlefish
茉莉花茶	*mòlì huāchá*	jasmine tea
牡丹	*mǔdān*	peony
墓地	*mùdì*	burial grounds
男厕	*náncè*	men's room
脑膜炎	*nǎomó yán*	meningitis
脑炎	*nǎoyán*	encephalitis
年糕	*niángāo*	glutinous rice cake
年画	*niánhuà*	New Year painting
牛肉	*niúròu*	beef
女厕	*nǚcè*	women's room
疟疾	*nüèjì*	malaria
藕	*ǒu*	lotus root
呕吐	*ǒutù*	vomit
排骨	*páigǔ*	sparerib

SUPPLEMENT

牌楼	*páilóu*	memorial arch
排球	*páiqiú*	volleyball
派出所	*pàichūsuǒ*	police station
盘尼西林	*pānníxīlín*	penicillin
螃蟹	*pángxiè*	crab
泡菜	*pàocài*	pickled vegetables
盆地	*péndì*	land basin
盆景	*pénjǐng*	bonsai
朋友	*péngyǒu*	friend
批发	*pīfā*	wholesale
霹雳舞	*pīliwǔ*	breakdancing
皮蛋	*pídàn*	thousand-year egg
皮肤科	*pífūkē*	dermatology department
琵琶	*pípá*	4-string lute
枇杷	*pípá*	loquat
皮下	*píxià*	hypodermic
皮鞋	*píxié*	leather shoes
皮影	*píyǐng*	shadow puppet
皮疹	*pízhěn*	rash
贫血症	*pínxuě zhèng*	anemia
评剧	*píngjù*	Pingju Opera
平原	*píngyuán*	plains
破伤风	*pò shāngfēng*	tetanus
葡萄	*pútáo*	grape
葡萄干	*pútáo gān*	raisin
葡萄糖	*pútáo táng*	glucose
普洱茶	*Pǔ'ěr chá*	Puer tea
普通舱	*pǔtōngcāng*	economy class
祁门红茶	*Qímén hóngchá*	Keemun tea
气喘	*qìchuǎn*	asthma
气功	*qìgōng*	breath energy exercise
千	*qiān*	thousand
千克	*qiānkè*	kilogram
签证	*qiānzhèng*	visa
蔷薇	*qiángwēi*	hedge rose
茄子	*qiézi*	eggplant
芹菜	*qíncài*	celery
青光眼	*qīngguāng yǎn*	glaucoma
青椒	*qīngjiāo*	green pepper
青稞	*qīngkē*	barley
青霉素	*qīngméisù*	pencillin

青蛙	*qīngwā*	frog
清真	*qīngzhēn*	Moslem
晴纶	*qínglún*	polyester
秋海棠	*qiūhǎitáng*	begonia
全身麻醉	*quánshēn mázuì*	general anesthesia
人民日报	***Rénmín Rìbào***	People's Daily
人参	*rénshēn*	ginseng
人造丝	*rénzào sī*	rayon
日报	*rìbào*	daily newspaper
榕树	*róngshù*	banyan tree
肉松	*ròusōng*	shredded dried meat
乳猪	*rǔzhū*	roast suckling pig
阮	*ruǎn*	Chinese banjo
软膏	*ruǎngāo*	ointment
软卧	*ruǎnwò*	soft-sleeper
软席	*ruǎnxí*	soft-seat
三弦琴	*sānxián qín*	3-string guitar
桑树	*sāngshù*	mulberry tree
嗓子	*sǎngzi*	throat; voice
瑟	*sè*	25-string zither
山羊	*shānyáng*	goat
山芋	*shānyù*	sweet potato
山楂	*shānzhā*	haw
鳝鱼	*shànyú*	eel
商店	*shāngdiàn*	shop
伤寒	*shānghán*	typhoid
伤口	*shāngkǒu*	wound (n)
烧饼	*shāobǐng*	sesame biscuit
蛇	*shé*	snake
猞猁	*shělì*	lynx
神经病学	*shénjīngbìng xué*	neurology
神经质	*shénjīngzhì*	neurosis
肾	*shèn*	kidney
升	*shēng*	liter
笙	*shēng*	Chinese mouth organ
生姜	*shēngjiāng*	ginger
省	*shěng*	province
师傅	*shīfu*	master worker
失眠	*shīmián*	insomnia
石版画	*shíbǎnhuà*	lithograph
实际	*shíjì*	practical, realistic

石榴	*shíliù*	pomegranate
食品店	*shípǐn diàn*	grocery store
食物中毒	*shíwù zhòng dú*	food poisoning
柿子	*shìzi*	persimmon
收款处	*shōukuǎnchù*	cashier's booth
首班车	*shǒu bān chē*	first bus or train
手风琴	*shǒufēngqín*	accordion
手术室	*shǒushù shì*	operation room
寿	*shòu*	symbol for longevity
寿眉茶	*Shòuméi chá*	White Peony tea
售票处	*shòupiào chù*	ticket office
书店	*shūdiàn*	bookstore
书记处	*shūjìchù*	secretariat
叔叔	*shūshu*	uncle
涮羊肉	*shuànyángròu*	Mongolian hot pot
水貂	*shuǐdiāo*	mink
水浮莲	*shuǐfúlián*	water lily
水饺	*shuǐjiǎo*	ravioli, boiled dumplings
水獭	*shuǐtǎ*	otter
水仙	*shuǐxiān*	narcissus
税	*shuì*	tax
睡前	*shuìqián*	before sleep
四合院	*sìhéyuàn*	traditional Chinese courtyard
四季豆	*sìjìdòu*	string bean
松	*sōng*	pine tree
松花蛋	*sōnghuādàn*	thousand-year egg
宿舍	*sùshè*	dormitory; housing
酸	*suān*	sore; sour
酸辣汤	*suānlà tāng*	hot-and-sour soup
酸奶	*suānnǎi*	yogurt
蒜	*suàn*	garlic
孙中山	*Sūn Zhōngshān*	Sun Yat-sen
唢呐	*suǒnà*	Chinese cornet
台风	*táifēng*	typhoon
太监	*tàijiān*	eunuch
滩羊	*tānyáng*	argali sheep
汤	*tāng*	soup
汤面	*tāngmiàn*	soup noodles

唐老鸭	*Tánglǎoyā*	Donald Duck
糖尿病	*tángniàobìng*	diabetes
桃子	*táozi*	peach
特快	*tèkuài*	express
疼	*téng*	pain
体温	*tǐwēn*	temperature
体育馆	*tǐyùguǎn*	gymnasium
甜菜	*tiáncài*	beet
铁观音茶	*Tiěguānyīn chá*	Iron Goddess of Mercy tea
同志	*tóngzhì*	comrade
痛苦	*tòngkǔ*	pain
头班车	*tóu bān chē*	first bus or train
头等舱	*tóuděngcāng*	first class
头晕	*tóuyūn*	dizzy
兔子	*tùzi*	rabbit
推拿	*tuīná*	massage
退热	*tuìrè*	antipyretic
吞咽	*tūnyàn*	swallow
外宾	*wàibīn*	foreign guest
外汇	*wàihuì*	foreign exchange certificate
外科	*wàikē*	surgery department
外用	*wàiyòng*	external use
豌豆黄	*wāndòu huáng*	pea-flour cake
万	*wàn*	ten thousand
危急	*wēijí*	critical
围棋	*wéiqí*	go
胃穿孔	*wèi chuānkǒng*	gastric perforation
胃疼	*wèiténg*	stomachache
胃炎	*wèiyán*	gastritis
蚊子	*wénzi*	mosquito
问讯处	*wènxún chù*	information desk
莴笋	*wōsǔn*	asparagus lettuce
乌龟	*wūguī*	tortoise
乌龙茶	*wūlóng chá*	oolong tea
乌贼	*wūzéi*	cuttlefish
无轨电车	*wúguǐ diànchē*	trolley
无花果	*wúhuāguǒ*	fig
梧桐树	*wútóngshù*	Chinese parasol tree
五粮液	*wǔliángyè*	five-grain liquor

SUPPLEMENT

武术	*wǔshù*	martial arts
舞厅	*wǔtīng*	dance hall
五线谱	*wǔxiàn pǔ*	5-line musical staff
希尔顿	*Xī'ěrdùn*	Hilton
西餐	*xīcān*	Western meal
稀饭	*xīfàn*	porridge, congee
西红柿	*xīhóngshì*	tomato
喜	*xǐ*	symbol for happiness
囍	*xǐ*	double happiness
喜来登	*Xǐláidēng*	Sheraton
喜玛拉雅山	*Xǐmǎlāyǎ shān*	Himalayas
虾	*xiā*	shrimp
咸鸭蛋	*xián yādàn*	salted duck egg
衔接航班	*xiánjiē hángbān*	connecting flight
县	*xiàn*	county
乡	*xiāng*	township
香菜	*xiāngcài*	coriander
香格里拉	*Xiānggélǐlā*	Shangri-La
香菇	*xiānggū*	black mushroom
香酥鸡	*xiāngsū jī*	fried crisp chicken
香酥鸭	*xiāngsū yā*	crispy duck
香油	*xiāngyóu*	sesame oil
香肠	*xiāngcháng*	sausage
象棋	*xiàngqí*	Chinese chess
相声	*xiàngsheng*	cross talk
箫	*xiāo*	vertical bamboo flute
消毒膏	*xiāodú gāo*	antiseptic cream
消化	*xiāohuà*	digestion
小笼包	*xiǎolóng bāo*	small steamed dumpling
小山羊皮	*xiǎoshānyáng pí*	kidskin
小熊猫	*xiǎoxióngmāo*	lesser panda
小羊皮	*xiǎoyáng pí*	lambskin
泻药	*xièyào*	cathartic
新石器时代	*xīn shíqì shídài*	Neolithic era
心绞痛	*xīnjiǎotòng*	angina pectoris
心理学	*xīnlǐxué*	psychology
心力衰竭	*xīnlì suāijié*	cardiac failure
心跳	*xīntiào*	palpitation
心脏病发作	*xīnzàngbìng fāzuò*	heart attack
腥红热	*xīnghóngrè*	scarlet fever
杏	*xìng*	apricot

幸福	xìngfú	happiness
杏仁	xìngrén	almond
杏仁茶	xìngrénchá	almond-flour tea
杏仁豆腐	xìngrén dòufu	almond gelatin
休克	xiūkè	shock
绣球	xiùqiú	geranium
岫玉	xiùyù	Manchurian jasper
宣纸	xuānzhǐ	rice paper
血	xuě	blood
血压	xuěyā	blood pressure
血型	xuèxíng	blood type
薰鱼	xūnyú	smoked fish
牙科医生	yákē yīshēng	dentist
亚麻布	yàmá bù	linen
腌黄瓜	yān huánggua	pickled cucumber
阉鸡	yānjī	capon
研究所	yánjiūsuǒ	research institute; graduate school
岩溶	yánróng	karst
眼科	yǎnkē	opthamology department
眼药水	yǎnyàoshuǐ	eye drops
咽	yàn	swallow
砚台	yàntai	ink slab
羊毛	yángmáo	wool
杨梅	yángméi	red bayberry
扬琴	yángqín	dulcimer
羊肉	yángròu	mutton
痒	yǎng	itch
氧气	yǎngqì	oxygen
样品	yàngpǐn	sample
腰鼓	yāogǔ	waist drum
腰果	yāoguǒ	cashew nut
腰疼	yāoténg	lumbago
药	yào	medicine
药方	yàofāng	prescription
药房	yàofáng	pharmacy
药丸	yàowán	pill
椰子	yēzi	coconut
夜班车	yèbān chē	night bus
腋下	yèxià	underarm

SUPPLEMENT

亿	yì	hundred million
译制片	yìzhì piàn	dubbed film
音乐厅	yīnyuè tīng	concert hall
银耳	yín'ěr	white edible fungus
银杏	yínxìng	ginkgo
饮料	yǐnliào	beverage
印泥	yìnní	red paste for seals
英里	yīnglǐ	mile
樱桃	yīngtáo	cherry
硬卧	yìngwò	hard-sleeper
硬坐	yìngzuò	hard-seat
油菜	yóucài	rape
邮局	yóujú	post office
邮票	yóupiào	postage stamp
油条	yóutiáo	fried cruller
鱿鱼	yóuyú	squid
柚子	yòuzi	pomelo
鱼	yú	fish
鱼翅汤	yúchì tāng	shark's fin soup
榆树	yúshù	elm tree
羽毛球	yǔmáoqiú	badminton
豫剧	yùjù	Henan Opera
芋头	yùtou	taro
鸳鸯	yuānyang	mandarin ducks
原作	yuánzuò	original
月季	yuèjì	Chinese rose
月经	yuèjīng	menstruation
越剧	yuèjù	Shaoxing Opera
粤剧	yuèjù	Cantonese Opera
月票	yuèpiào	monthly ticket
月琴	yuèqín	4-string mandolin
芸豆	yúndòu	kidney bean
枣	zǎo	date
澡堂	zǎotáng	bathhouse
榨菜	zhàcài	hot pickled mustard tuber
占线	zhànxiàn	busy line
樟树	zhāngshù	camphor tree
招待所	zhāodàisuǒ	guesthouse
针灸	zhēnjiǔ	acupuncture
真丝	zhēnsī	silk

珍珠	*zhēnzhū*	pearl
诊断	*zhěnduàn*	diagnosis
镇	*zhèn*	town
镇静剂	*zhènjìngjì*	tranquilizer
筝	*zhēng*	many-stringed zither
政治局	*zhèngzhìjú*	political bureau
症状	*zhèngzhuàng*	symptom
支气管炎	*zhīqìguǎn yán*	bronchitis
止疼药	*zhǐténg yào*	pain-killer
中餐	*zhōngcān*	Chinese meal
钟楼	*zhōnglóu*	bell tower
中药	*zhōngyào*	traditional Chinese medicine
肿胀	*zhǒngzhàng*	swelling
中暑	*zhòngshǔ*	sunstroke
粥	*zhōu*	porridge, congee
珠穆朗玛峰	*Zhūmùlángmǎ fēng*	Mount Everest
猪肉	*zhūròu*	pork
竹笋	*zhúsǔn*	bamboo shoot
注射	*zhùshè*	injection
住院处	*zhùyuàn chù*	inpatient department
紫貂	*zǐdiāo*	sable
足球	*zúqiú*	soccer
钻石	*zuànshí*	diamond

APPENDIX A

Numbers and Quantities

Cardinal Numbers

Numeral			Comments
0	零	*líng*	
1	一	*yī* *	*1 is read as *yāo* when stating a phone number, room number, bus number, and such identifications.
2	二	*èr* **	
3	三	*sān*	
4	四	*sì*	
5	五	*wǔ*	**2 is usually read as *liǎng* when referring to quantity. For example, "two people" would be *liǎng gè rén*.
6	六	*liù*	
7	七	*qī*	
8	八	*bā*	
9	九	*jiǔ*	
10	十	*shí*	
20	二十	*èrshí*	two tens
30	三十	*sānshí*	three tens
40...	四十	*sìshí*...	four tens...
11	十一	*shíyī*	ten and one
12	十二	*shí'èr*	ten and two
13...	十三	*shísān*...	ten and three...
21	二十一	*èrshí yī*	twenty and one
22	二十二	*èrshí èr*	twenty and two
23...	二十三	*èrshí sān*...	twenty and three...
100	百	*bǎi*	
1,000	千	*qiān*	
10,000	万	*wàn*	
1,000,000	百万	*bǎiwàn*	

Ordinal Numbers

Ordinal numbers are formed by inserting *dì* in front of the number.

first	*dìyī*	第一
second	*dì'èr*	第二
third...	*dìsān...*	第三
first one	*dìyī gè*	第一个
first time	*dìyī cì*	第一次

Fractions

Except for one-half, *yí bàn,* fractions are formed in the pattern (D) *fēnzhī* (N) with D being the denominator and N the numerator.

Examples:

1/3	*sān fēnzhī yī*	三分之一
1/4	*sì fēnzhī yī*	四分之一
3/4	*sì fēnzhī sān*	四分之三
2/5	*wǔ fēnzhī èr*	五分之二

Percentages

To form a percentage, use the pattern *bǎi fēnzhī* (P) with P being the percentage.

Examples:

25%	*bǎi fēnzhī èrshí wǔ*	百分之二十五
80%	*bǎi fēnzhībāshí*	百分之八十
100%	*bǎi fēnzhī yìbǎi*	百分之一百

Measure Words

Measure Word		What It Modifies	Examples
bǎ	把	knives, chairs, keys	*sān bǎ dāo* (3 knives) *yì bǎ yǐzi* (a chair)
běn	本	books	*yì běn xiǎoshuō* (a novel) *liǎng běn zìdiǎn* (2 dictionaries)
duì	对	pairs, couples	*yí duì huāpíng* (a pair of vases) *sān duì fūfù* (3 married couples)
fèn	份	portions, printed matter, newspapers	*yí fèn "Zhōngguó Rìbào"* (a copy of *China Daily*)
fēng	封	letters (mail)	*liǎng fēng xìn* (2 letters)
gè	个	most things	*sān gè rén* (3 people) *yí gè píngguǒ* (an apple) *wǔ gè xīngqī* (5 weeks)
jiān	间	rooms	*liǎng jiān wòshì* (2 bedrooms)
jiàn	件	clothing, suitcases	*yí jiàn chènshān* (a shirt) *liǎng jiàn xíngli* (2 suitcases)
kē	棵	trees	*yì kē sōngshù* (a pine tree)
kuài	块	rectangular objects, money	*yí kuài féizào* (a bar of soap) *sì kuài miànbāo* (4 slices of bread) *shí kuài qián* (10 yuan)

continued

APPENDIX B

liàng	辆	vehicles	*yí liàng zìxíngchē* (a bicycle)
			liǎng liàng qìchē (2 cars)
pán	盘	flat, circular objects	*zhèi pán cídài* (this tape cassette)
			wǔ pán cài (5 dishes of food)
shuāng	双	pairs related to hands and feet	*yì shuāng píxié* (a pair of leather shoes)
			sì shuāng shǒutào (4 pairs of gloves)
tái	台	machines	*yì tái dǎzìjī* (a typewriter)
			yì tái jìsuànjī (a computer)
tiáo	条	long, linear objects	*yì tiáo kùzi* (a pair of pants)
			yì tiáo jiē (a street)
			sān tiáo yú (3 fish)
zhāng	张	sheets, such as paper, tickets, photos, maps	*liǎng zhāng piào* (2 tickets)
			jǐ zhāng zhǐ (some sheets of paper)
zhī	只	animals	*sān zhī niǎo* (3 birds)
			yì zhī lǎohǔ (a tiger)
zhī	支	writing tools	*yì zhī máobǐ* (a Chinese brush)
			sān zhī gāngbǐ (3 fountain pens)

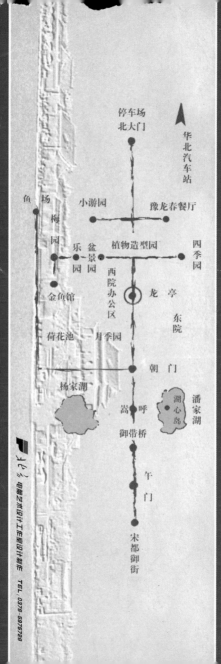

开封龙亭公园

APPENDIX C

Expressions of Time

Divisions of the Day

morning	zǎoshang, zǎochen	早上, 早晨
mid-morning	shàngwǔ	上午
noon	zhōngwǔ	中午
afternoon	xiàwǔ	下午
evening	wǎnshang	晚上
night	yèlǐ	夜里

Hours and Minutes

hour	xiǎoshí, zhōngtóu	小时, 钟头
half	bàn	半
quarter	kè	刻
o'clock	diǎn, diǎnzhōng	点, 点钟
minute	fēn, fēnzhōng	分, 分钟
less	chà	差

Examples:

3 hours	sān gè xiǎoshí
3 ½ hours	sān gè bàn xiǎoshí
8:00	bādiǎn, bā diǎnzhōng
8:05	bā diǎn líng wǔ
8:10	bā diǎn shí fēn
8:15	bā diǎn yí kè
8:30	bā diǎn bàn
8:50	bā diǎn wǔshí, jiǔ diǎn chà shí fēn
9:00 am	zǎoshang jiǔ diǎn
9:00 pm	wǎnshang jiǔ diǎn
2:00 pm	xiàwǔ liǎng diǎn
2:00 am	yèlǐ liǎng diǎn

APPENDIX D

Conversion Charts

Measures

The metric system is widely used in China, along with a few traditional Chinese units of measure. The chart below gives rough equivalences among the various systems. The Chinese translations of the metric and American units, such as *shēng* for liter, can be found in the dictionary.

Chinese Unit	Metric Unit	American Unit
Length		
	1 cm	.4 in
	2.5 cm	1 in
	30.5 cm	1 ft
1 *chǐ* 尺	33.3 cm	13.1 in
	91.4 cm	1 yd
3 *chǐ*	1 m	39.4 in
1 *lǐ* 里	.5 km	.3 mi
2 *lǐ*	1 km	.6 mi
	1.6 km	1 mi
Area		
	6.5 sq cm	1 sq in
	929 sq cm	1 sq ft
	.8 sq m	1 sq yd
	1 sq m	1550 sq in
1 *mǔ* 亩	674.5 sq m	807 sq yd
6 *mǔ*	4,047 sq m	1 acre
15 *mǔ*	1 ha	2.5 acres
	1 sq km	.4 sq mi
	2.6 sq km	1 sq mi

Weight

1 *qián* 钱	5g	.2 oz
	28.4 g	1 oz
1 *liǎng* 两	50 g	1.8 oz
	454 g	1 lb
1 *jīn* 斤	500 g	1.1 lb
2 *jīn*	1 kg	2.2 lb
	.9 MT	1 ton
2,000 *jīn*	1 MT	2,204.6 lb

Capacity

1 cl	.3 fl oz	1.1 l	1 qt (dry)
47.3 cl	1 pt (fl)	3.8 l	1 gal (fl)
55 cl	1 pt (dry)	8.8 l	1 pk
94.6 cl	1 qt (fl)	35.2 l	1 bu
1 l	1.1 qt (fl)	1 hl	2.8 bu
1 l	.9 qt (dry)		

Temperature

	°C	°F
	35	95
	30	86
	25	77
	20	68
To calculate the Fahrenheit	15	59
equivalent of a centigrade	10	50
temperature, use this formula:	5	41
$F = 32 + 1.8 C$	0	32
	-5	23
	-10	14
	-15	5
	-20	-4

APPENDIX E

Money

Chinese Currency

The Chinese currency is called *rénmínbì* (RMB), with the basic unit being the *yuán* (¥). One-tenth of a yuan is called a *jiǎo*. One-hundredth of a yuan is called a *fēn*.

In spoken Chinese, a yuan is often called a *kuài* and a jiao is called a *máo*. When stating a price, the last identifying word "mao" or "fen" is left out.

Examples:

¥15.00	*shíwǔ kuài*
¥15.65	*shíwǔ kuài liù máo wǔ* (no "fen")
¥ 1.50	*yí kuài wǔ* (no "mao")
¥ .30	*sān máo*
¥ .32	*sān máo èr* (no "fen")
¥ .02	*liǎng fēn*

Foreign Currencies

US dollar	*Měiyuán*	美元
Canadian dollar	*Jiāyuán*	加元
Australian dollar	*Àoyuán*	澳元
New Zealand dollar	*Xīnxīlán yuán*	新西兰元
Pound sterling	*Yīngbàng*	英镑
Japanese yen	*Rìyuán*	日元
Hong Kong dollar	*Gǎngbì*	港币

Key Words:

currency	*bì*	币	mark	*mǎkè*	马克
dollar	*yuán*	元	peso	*bǐsuǒ*	比索
franc	*fǎláng*	法郎	pound	*bàng*	镑
lira	*lǐlā*	里拉	rupee	*lúbǐ*	卢比

Place Names

Major Administrative Divisions

China is divided into 23 provinces, 5 autonomous regions, and 3 municipalities directly under the Central Government.

Municipalities under the Central Government

北京	*Běijīng*
上海	*Shànghǎi*
天津	*Tiānjīn*

Autonomous Regions

广西	*Guǎngxī* (Zhuang Autonomous Region)
内蒙古	*Nèi Měnggǔ* (Inner Mongolia)
宁夏	*Níngxià* (Hui Autonomous Region)
新疆	*Xīnjiāng* (Uygur Autonomous Region)
西藏	*Xīzàng* (Tibet)

Provinces

安徽	*Ānhuī*	江西	*Jiāngxī*
福建	*Fújiàn*	吉林	*Jílín*
甘肃	*Gānsù*	辽宁	*Liáoníng*
广东	*Guǎngdōng*	青海	*Qīnghǎi*
贵州	*Guìzhōu*	山东	*Shāndōng*
海南	*Hǎinán*	山西	*Shānxī*
河北	*Héběi*	陕西 ·	*Shǎnxī* (Shaanxi)
河南	*Hénán*		
黑龙江	*Hēilóngjiāng*	·四川	*Sìchuān*
湖北	*Húběi*	台湾	*Táiwān*
湖南	*Húnán*	云南	*Yúnnán*
江苏	*Jiāngsū*	浙江	*Zhèjiāng*

Cities of Interest

Below is a selected list of cities with historic, cultural, or economic significance.

鞍山	Ānshān	江陵	Jiānglíng
包头	Bāotóu	景德镇	Jǐngdézhèn
保定	Bǎodìng	景洪	Jǐnghóng
北戴河	Běidàihé	喀什	Kāshí (Kashgar)
北京	Běijīng		
长春	Chángchūn	开封	Kāifēng
长沙	Chángshā	昆明	Kūnmíng
承德	Chéngdé	拉萨	Lāsà (Lhasa)
成都	Chéngdū	兰州	Lánzhōu
重庆	Chóngqìng	洛阳	Luòyáng
大理	Dàlǐ	南昌	Nánchāng
大连	Dàlián	南京	Nánjīng
大同	Dàtóng	南宁	Nánníng
大足	Dàzú	宁波	Níngbō
敦煌	Dūnhuáng	青岛	Qīngdǎo
佛山	Fóshān	曲阜	Qūfù
抚顺	Fǔshùn	泉州	Quánzhōu
福州	Fúzhōu	日喀则	Rìkezé (Shigatse, Xigaze)
格尔木	Gé'ěrmù (Golmud)		
广州	Guǎngzhōu (Canton)	上海	Shànghǎi
		韶山	Sháoshān
桂林	Guìlín	绍兴	Shàoxīng
哈尔滨	Hā'ěrbīn (Harbin)	深圳	Shēnzhèn
		沈阳	Shěnyáng
海口	Hǎikǒu	石家庄	Shíjiāzhuāng
杭州	Hángzhōu	苏州	Sūzhōu
合肥	Héféi	太原	Tàiyuán
呼和浩特	Hūhéhàotè (Hohhot)	天津	Tiānjīn
		吐鲁番	Tǔlǔfān (Turfan)
		温州	Wēnzhōu

乌鲁木齐	*Wūlǔmùqí* (Urumqi)	延安	*Yán'ān*
无锡	*Wúxī*	扬州	*Yángzhōu*
武汉	*Wǔhàn*	宜昌	*Yíchāng*
西安	*Xī'ān*	岳阳	*Yuèyáng*
西宁	*Xīníng*	肇庆	*Zhàoqìng*
厦门	*Xiàmén* (Amoy)	镇江	*Zhènjiāng*
		郑州	*Zhèngzhōu*

APPENDIX G

Dynasties

The Chinese dynasties are outlined here in brief.

Xia 夏		ca 21st - 16th cent BC
Shang 商		ca 16th - 11th cent BC
Zhou 周		ca 11th cent - 221 BC
Western Zhou		
Eastern Zhou		
Spring and Autumn		
Warring States		
Qin 秦		221-207 BC
Han 汉		206 BC—AD 220
Western Han		
Eastern Han		
Three Kingdoms 三国		220-280
Western Jin 西晋		265-316
Eastern Jin 东晋		317-420
Northern and Southern Dynasties 南北朝		420-581
Sui 隋		581-618
Tang 唐		618-907
Five Dynasties 五代		907-960
Song 宋		960-1279
Northern Song		
Southern Song		
		1271-1368
		1368-1644
		1644-1911

APPENDIX H

Family Relations

In Chinese, addressing relatives is not just a matter of calling "aunt" or "uncle"—you have to specify whether the relative is on your mother or father's side and sometimes the relative's age in respect to yourself or your parent.

Paternal Relatives

爷爷	yéye	grandfather
奶奶	nǎinai	grandmother
伯伯	bóbo	uncle (father's older brother)
伯母	bómǔ	his wife
叔叔	shūshu	uncle (father's younger brother)
婶婶	shěnshen	his wife
姑姑	gūgu	aunt (father's sister)
姑夫	gūfu	her husband
堂哥	táng gē	older boy cousin
堂弟	táng dì	younger boy cousin
堂姐	táng jiě	older girl cousin
堂妹	táng mèi	younger girl cousin

Maternal Relatives

姥爷, 外公	lǎoye, wàigōng	grandfather
姥姥, 外婆	lǎolao, wàipó	grandmother
姨姨	yíyi	aunt (mother's sister)
姨夫	yífu	her husband
舅舅	jiùjiu	uncle (mother's brother)
舅妈	jiùmā	his wife
表哥	biǎo gē	older boy cousin
表弟	biǎo dì	younger boy cousin
表姐	biǎo jiě	older girl cousin
表妹	biǎo mèi	younger girl cousin

APPENDIX H

Immediate Family

爸爸	bàba	father
妈妈	māma	mother
哥哥	gēge	older brother
嫂子	sǎozi	his wife
弟弟	dìdi	younger brother
弟妹, 弟媳	dìmèi, dìxí	his wife
姐姐	jiějie	older sister
姐夫	jiěfu	her husband
妹妹	mèimei	younger sister
妹夫	mèifu	her husband
女儿	nǚér	daughter
女婿	nǚxu	son-in-law
儿子	érzi	son
媳妇	xífù	daughter-in-law
孙子	sūnzi	grandson (son's son)
孙女	sūnnǚ	granddaughter (son's daughter)
外孙	wàisūn	grandson (daughter's son)
外孙女	wàisūnnǚ	granddaughter (daughter's daughter)

continued

旅游会话

陈蒙惠 编著
殷 边

*

外文出版社出版

（中国北京百万庄路 24 号）

华利国际合营印刷有限公司印刷

中国国际图书贸易总公司

（中国国际书店）发行

北京 399 信箱

1988 年（36 开）第一版

1990 年第二次印刷

（英）

ISBN 7—119—00557—X/H·74

00840

9-CE-2297P